QUICKIES TOO

QUICKIES TOO

DON P. MARQUESS

To order additional copies of this book, contact:
Xlibris
844-714-8691
www.Xlibris.com
Orders@Xlibris.com
852142

CONTENTS

PREFACE

Egad! I am eighty-two years old and writing my second book? My intention in writing these stories is only to entertain. There are no murders, no politics, no villains, no controversies, no sex (now that I mentioned all the things my book isn't, I wonder why anyone would want to read this book …), but anyway, you purchased it and there is no turning back!

These are all very true stories just written to make the reader smile. One of my English professors termed my writing a "conversational prose," sayin' that my stories are written as if I am talking directly to the reader.

As I approach the half way point of my life, I feel compelled to relate these very humorous events in my life. When I think of them again, I tend to chuckle and wish to share these moments with the reader. With all the unhappy and dramatic events occurring in our world today, I think of the funny things in life, and they take me away from the drama of the world and give me comfort and laughter. My good friend, Hall of Fame broadcaster, Jack Buck, every Saturday morning when I was with him in his kitchen, no matter what his ailments were (he had Parkinson's, a pacemaker, cancer, and was an insulin-dependent diabetic), he would always look at the funny side of life and keep me laughing with his take on whatever the situation happened to be. He told me he was anxious to get Alzheimer's because then he would forget he had Parkinson's. No matter what, Jack always found humor in the darkest situations.

My only intention of writing these very short stories is that after a difficult day working, or even a bad day on the golf course, the reader will take a few minutes to read these true events and hopefully lighten a day's tensions. I am not preaching nor attempting to persuade you to do anything other than to take a few moments to read my stories, then relax and smile for a while.

CHAPTER 1

The Value of Autographs

The Chicago Cubs call it the Cubs Convention, the Boston Red Sox call it the Red Sox Winter Weekend, the Yankees call it Yankee's Fan Fest—they are all mid-winter baseball fan gatherings. At these fests, baseball fans come together to get ready for the coming baseball season. Baseball fans are unrelenting in their desire to see and do anything connected with their favorite sport. At these events, anything even remotely concerned with baseball is on display in booths with vendors hoping to tempt fans to purchase their wares.

The St. Louis Cardinals call their fan fest the Winter Warmup. In 1999, which was after Mark McGwire broke the Roger Maris's record of sixty-one home runs, and totally shattering it with seventy home runs, we had a booth for our baseball "art." Mark McGwire was attending the Winter Warmup. What a terrific event for Cardinals's fans.

I was very fortunate in securing the exclusive art photographic rights to the seventieth home run baseball. I produced seventy Cibachrome 30" x 40" prints that sold for $2,500 each, and seven thousand 18" x 24" poster prints that were priced at $70.00 each. That ball was auctioned at Gurnsey's in New York and purchased by cartoonist Todd McFarlane for $3.14 million. With Mark McGwire in attendance and signing his autograph on items brought by fans, this was indeed a stand out event for Cardinals's fans. My prints were offered in our booth with Phil Ozersky (who caught the ball), and I'm signing the prints. People lined up were twenty-five or so deep and anxious to get the print of the actual ball Mark McGwire hit for number 70.

Darlene Williams, our gallery curator, was assisting in the booth taking the money and placing the prints in the large envelopes to take to Mark McGwire for his autograph. This was indeed an event for the ages. Every purchaser seemed thrilled to have the photographer and the man who caught the ball signing the prints for Mark to sign.

With one exception . . .

The next person in line to purchase the print asked if I had to sign the print. I was amazed that someone wasn't thrilled that I was signing the photo that I created.

I said, "If I signed it, it would cost $70, if I didn't sign it, it would cost $130."

Darlene Williams heard me tell him that, and exploded with laughter.

The purchaser, who apparently had zero sense of humor, looked at me very seriously and said, "Well then, could you sign it on the back?"

It was then established that my autograph devalues anything I sign.

(Think twice before getting a signed copy of this book.)

CHAPTER 2

Man Mountain Oscar

We lived on a street named Oleatha in Southwest St. Louis that had many houses very close together with meticulously manicured lawns. This was 1950, and I was nine years old. Running behind all the houses on the block was an alley separating the houses on the next block from the houses on our block. Each house had an ashpit where the ashes from our coal furnaces were stored, and several times during the winter season, ashpit cleaners would come down the alley and empty the ashes for a $5.00 or so charge. An ashpit was a roughly 4' x 4' heavy-duty structure built with about 5" thick of concrete and stood about 4 1/2' tall. It was a very sturdy structure. My job was to fill the coal scuttle periodically with the ashes from the coal furnace and empty them in the ashpit. I also was charged with filling the hopper with coal from the coal bin to keep the coal cooking. I felt very proud that I had such important responsibilities. Our family could freeze if I didn't keep that hopper loaded.

Then in a very sad moment occurred, the city of St. Louis passed an ordinance that all ashpits had to be removed. My job was over. Then came a raft of carpetbaggers and scalawags offering to destroy and haul away the pits for some outrageous price, or at least that is what my daddy said. That was indeed "the pits" for me. I loved that pit and enjoyed my responsibility as well. My father had a man that worked for him named Oscar Jarret who said he would remove it for a much more reasonable price. His cousin had a flatbed truck that he could borrow and save my dad lots of money . . . deal done.

Oscar had deep blue-black skin with the most muscled arms and shoulders that I had ever seen. Hercules would be envious. It was a Saturday when Oscar the Giant came to destroy our ashpit, but our house was in the center of the block, and while driving down our alley, he got two more ashpit removing jobs. By the time he reached our house, he had already a couple of destroyed ashpits on his cousin's flatbed.

I was so excited to see Oscar and his unbelievable muscles. I told many of my friends on the block that they had to come and see this incredibly powerful man. I felt that Oscar could star in any movie and wipe out every villain, and then blow the smoke off his hands in victory. We all gathered around the ashpit, awaiting Oscar's arrival. When he got there, I could almost hear the trumpets heralding his arrival. Oscar was indeed a specimen of wonder. He was a star, as was I for bringing him.

Oscar smiled at his admiring audience of marveling ten year olds, and removed his sledgehammer of destruction and struck the first damaging blow. It took several swings, but the heavily reinforced concrete was no match for Oscar. The side of the pit started to give way. My neighborhood friends couldn't believe the strength that Oscar had. His muscles bulged, and the veins in his neck became enlarged with each piece of broken concrete that Oscar hurled on to his cousin's truck. The more we marveled and cheered, the bigger the chunk he hurled. Oscar, being a true showman and loving the cheering praise, grabbed the biggest piece of all, raised it over his sweat-glistening shoulders, grunted with an explosive *oomph*, and threw it high in the air to land on the concrete laden bed of the truck. It landed with a thundering thump, and as Oscar was taking additional bows for his performance, there was another thundering thump. The axle on the truck split in half and the flatbed crashed to the ground. Oscar was out of business the same day he entered it.

His fans, all of my friends, and some I had never seen before cheered and threw flowers to him, and yelled "Encore, Encore." Well, not really, but if we knew the word we would have. Alley traffic came to a halt for several days until the broken truck and broken concrete rubble were removed. To this day, that last piece of concrete exists in the Hall of Fame of Ashpit Chunks. Nevertheless, I remained the neighborhood hero for years for bringing Man Mountain Oscar to our alley. Every now and then, I still bask in the glory of my accomplishment!

CHAPTER 3

The Book of Knowledge

The Conners family that lived across the street from our house had a full set of *Encyclopedia Britannica*. My elementary school, St. Joan of Arc, had the *World Book Encyclopedia*. Tommy Long's family had something called *Americana*, if I remember correctly. We had the *Book of Knowledge* encyclopedia, which my parents thought was the very accurate "Book of the Cat's Meow." I enjoyed reading the *World Book Encyclopedia* at school much more than any of the other publications. (I don't know if it was the type of printing, the font, or the layout, but it was my favorite to read during open time in the school day). Nevertheless, even as a fifth grader, I enjoyed reading useless information, and the encyclopedia at home was a good source for collecting information as well.

Our *Book of Knowledge* set was twenty plus volumes and contained many pages of interesting information. In later years, that information had gained the term "trivia," and I loved it then as I do today. One day as I was reading from our set of *The Book of Knowledge*, there was a story about how the ancient Egyptians measured the height of tall things that were too tall to measure with arms stretched to the max. I don't remember much about it other than it was done in Aswan or Alexandria with a pole of a known length. The information was that someone took that pole of which the length was known (let's say ten feet), placed it straight up in the ground, and measured the shadow it cast. So if the shadow was two feet, one-fifth of the length of the known pole, then the shadow cast by any tall building or structure was simply five times the length of the shadow. How neat was that?

I have been worried and greatly fearful of tornadoes ever since I saw that deadly one in the *Wizard of Oz*. That and also the stories my grandmother told me about her brother, Douglas Chamblin, who was a detective with the St. Louis police force, and who, at the age of thirty-six, was killed in the line of duty in 1927 from a deadly tornado when it collapsed a tall building that crushed him. At my age of ten years old, I had several frightful dreams that I, like Dorothy and my great uncle, would be blown to the heavens, or crushed by a tornado while I was sleeping snugly in my bed.

There was a giant oak tree in our neighbor's backyard across the alley that had me worried that someday, during a tornado, it would fall onto my room. My room was a remodeled and closed-in sunporch in the back end of our house. I loved that room, and while it was being enclosed and created as a year-round room, my mom and dad let me pick out the knotty pine walls and the burgundy vinyl tile for the floor. It was the first time I had my very own and super special room. But what if that giant oak tree fell on it and crushed it along with me? I now had the information to simply determine just where that devastation from the giant oak tree would hit.

So at two in the afternoon one day, I took a yardstick to our driveway and measured the length of the shadow. I didn't want to sink it in the ground because that would adversely affect the exposed length and mess up the equation. Fortunately, the concrete on our driveway was a flat surface, enabling me to get an accurate reading of the length of the shadow. I took several loose bricks from the garage (my dad was in the brick supply business, so we always had some laying around) and tried to support the yardstick. This took many attempts, as the yardstick needed support from at least three sides to keep it from falling over before I could measure the shadow. In the meantime, time was passing and it was no longer 2:00 p.m. It was getting close to 2:30 p.m., but I measured the shadow anyway and got my equation. Luckily the shadow was about one foot, approximately one-third of the length of the yardstick. Now I could determine the height of the Killer Oak and just how much peril my room and I were in.

I crossed our yard and searched for the end of the shadow of the tree. I found where the last leaf was located in the shadow and marked it with my pocketknife. That shadow ended at our side of the fence in our back yard. Now, all I had to do was measure the length of that shadow from the base of the tree, multiply it by three, and I would know what would happen to my room if the tornado hit that tree. My measuring tool was that yardstick, the length of which was constant; however, the time was not constant, as it was now close to 3:00 p.m., changing the length of that shadow. But that didn't matter to me . . . I had my equation.

As the shadow lengthened and the time passed, it changed the equation. But at ten years old, I didn't realize that and I proceeded. The tree was on the corner of the neighbor's property around seven or eight feet from their fence line. I had my yardstick for precise measurement, but I had to set the yardstick, starting at the base of the oak, going through the back fence, and going out their back gate to get to the yardstick, and continue my exact measurement.

I crossed the alley, set the yardstick through an opening at the base of our wire fence, and went around through the gate to reach the yardstick. It was the eighteenth yardstick, fifty-four feet so far. I looked for my pocketknife in the grass but couldn't locate it; and there on the other side of our backyard was my dog, Sarge nibbling on my pocket knife. Sarge was a great dog and behaved very well, so I called him to come to me and bring my knife. He brought it over. I asked him where he got it, but he didn't respond, so I just used my memory to find the exact spot for my "perfect" measurement. I determined that the shadow ended at about the twelfth yardstick, so that tree was 36' x 3', making the tree 108 feet tall, which is almost an eleven story building. There must have been something wrong with my exact and very accurate measurements because that must have been a world record oak tree. Nevertheless, I continued. Now with this exact height of the mighty oak, I returned to the base of the tree and started measuring by thirty-six yardsticks to get to 108 feet inside our house. (This was also a great variable, as I had to go through the back steps and estimate just where that yardstick would land as it passed through the walls). I figured that if my measurement was correct (why wouldn't it be?), my room would be totally gone by that tree falling. That measurement took me inside our house, just past the dining room table. My measuring ended at around 6:00 p.m., and my quest was complete and very accurate(?). Whenever bad weather was forecast, I ran to the dining room past the table for safe harbor, and I knew that if my room was obliterated, I would survive whatever Mother Nature threw at our house. Recently I returned to my boyhood home, and the tree was still standing as well as my room in the back of our house. An entire afternoon of my childhood *wasted*!

At 2:00 a.m. on February 10, 1959, an F4 tornado hit St. Louis, killing twenty-one people, injuring 358 people, and leaving 1,400 people homeless, all about five miles from my room on the back of the house, and I, being eighteen years old and fast asleep in my bed, slept through it!

Chapter 4

Creepy, Crawly Reptiles

Not very far from our house was Kenrick Seminary, which occupied a very large tract of land with densely packed trees and many pathways. The property housed the lower school that had a very impressive dome and steeple, while the upper school had an extremely dignified appearance with several squared off towers of dusty orange brick. The entire property was enormous. As we kids in the area could get into the compound and ride bikes on the paths approaching the seminary buildings, there was a permanent hobo camp with five or six denizens of the sacred forest. That encampment was apparently just outside the seminary property line. It didn't matter to us kids. We crossed the line and entered at will. It was indeed a magical place that was really exciting for us to visit . . . as long as we didn't get caught. When we did get caught, we were told by a security guard that it was private property and we had to leave. Most of the time we didn't leave, and we continued to explore.

At the edge of this forest was a large pond surrounded with strange and exotic elephant ear plants, and those cat of nine tails things. Large black birds with bright red under wings, that I only saw there to this very day, made that pond a very special place indeed. Also, with patience and intense searching, baby toads and little squirmy garter snakes could be found.

On many occasions, I would catch a tiny toad or two and take them home as pets until they hopped away and escaped. My brother, ten years older and many inches taller, 6'5", was a big sissy about my captures and didn't want to see them at all. One day in my searching around this pond, I found four little garter snakes. And being eight years old—and I guess a little devilish regarding my brother—brought the four garter snakes home, wrapped them around my fingers, and went through the house, seeking my brother. He was in the air-conditioned room in the house reading. I had my snake-covered fingers behind my back, got his attention, brought my fingers to within inches of his face, and said, "Hi, brother." He screamed, jumped off his chair, and his 6'5" body almost hit the ceiling! It was such a wonderful moment for a little kid to control such a giant. I don't think he ever fully recovered.

One day, while playing in the alley behind our house, I found a turtle heading with the speed of a snail crossing the alley. That turtle became my pet. I picked him up (don't really know if it was a him or a her, I guess only another turtle could tell) and brought him to our basement. There is not much a boy can do with a turtle, except marvel at the uniqueness of such a helmeted beast. They don't meow or bark and mostly appear disinterested in the goings on around them. They just hide their heads in their shell and poke them out occasionally, get bored, and go back in their shell to do nothing. However, this was *my* turtle and I loved him.

Days later, while playing in the alley, I saw another turtle traveling at breakneck speed across the alley. I outran him, captured him, and took him to the basement! I now had a companion for my turtle. Maybe it was a female, and I would end up with a real flock of turtles. How great was that. A few days later, there was another turtle in our back yard, which I, now with such great experience in turtle capturing, grabbed him and carried him to our turtle haven in the basement. The two other turtles would have a new playmate! I was thrilled. The next day, I went downstairs to see my turtle harvest and couldn't find even one. I searched everywhere. No turtles. I looked in the coal bin, looked behind the washer and dryer, but not even one turtle to be found. My mom had a closet in the basement where she put her canned jams and jellies. I thought maybe the turtle family had somehow gotten in there and were feasting on crabapple jam, but no luck. My three turtles had vanished never to be seen again!

Years later, many years later, my brother's best friend, Attorney John Healy, told me what happened to my pet turtles.

There was *only* one turtle! My big squeamish brother discovered my turtle, got the coal shovel, and scooped up my turtle and put him in the alley. I found him again, thought he was another turtle, and brought him downstairs. Same story once again. My brother found that damn turtle again and shoveled him off once more. My third turtle finally aggravated him to the point of shoveling him to neighborhoods unknown (or maybe even worse) and ended my turtle collection forever.

CHAPTER 5

Left-Handed (Like It Or Not)

I was born in November 1940 on the twenty-sixth of the month as a surprise Thanksgiving gift to my parents. I have an excellent memory; however, I really don't remember much about that occasion in the hospital, other than it was very dark then very bright. Even in 1940, St. Luke's Hospital had a very bright lighting system. After several days of rest, my mom and dad drove me home in his 1936 Ford coupe. When we reached home, I was placed in my crib and given a blue rattle. (That, among other things, told me that I was a booming baby boy). I grabbed that noisy instrument with my left hand, and it was to remain there forever. I was left-handed! A malady remaining to this very day.

My daddy was Methodist and my mother was Catholic, but according to the agreement between them, their children were to be raised and educated Catholic. I was to be baptized months later at a new church named St. Joan of Arc. As a matter of fact, I was to be the first baptism there. But according to my mom, I had some sort of bodily function mishap and some girl took my place. Nevertheless, 1 was the first boy baptized at St. Joan of Arc. Sadly for the world, I remained left-handed. With the world population admitting that only 8 percent or so of the world contains the outcast lefties.(It is probably a little over 10 percent, but the World Census Organization doesn't wish to own up to that many shortcomings.) The Catholic Church and its educational nuns tried desperately to correct my malfunction.

Crayon and triangle instructors in Miss Fairbanks Nursery School seemed not to notice the affliction. I still received the coveted gold star on my forehead for my stick tapping and triangle musical accomplishments. However, when I became a first grader at St. Gabriel's Elementary, it was an entirely different situation as I was moving on to higher education. Sister Mary DeSales and all of the other nuns just would not tolerate such an affliction. The bloody messes of my left hand became very painful. The penmanship portion of my education became increasingly difficult. Anytime I was supposed to print anything, my right hand would not participate. If I were lucky enough to print an A, B, C, or the severely challenging T or F by using my left hand, everything was OK. However, if I were caught using such a devious method, Sister would demand that I would present my left hand for flogging with her yardstick.

Moving on to the next educational level of second grade, I became increasingly intolerant of such corporal punishment. One day, when Sister Mary Pure (I think that was her name, although I may have a cloudy recollection) stood with her disapproving glare while holding the yardstick of death and said, "Marquess, hold out you hand." I didn't. She said it even louder and much more threatening. "Marquess, hold out your hand NOW!"

In a momentary loss of my mind, I grabbed the yardstick.

The entire second grade class said, "Ooogh."

I felt expulsion and great embarrassment that would no doubt ruin my educational process. Sister Mary Pure led me down the hall to see Father Steck. Yikes!

She took me into his office, sat me down in a chair, facing father, then left to return to the right-handed students.

I sat in fear as Father Steck looked at me and said, "Donny, you are left-handed, don't worry about it, I will handle it with Sister."

Sister, sadly for her, had to break her daily habit of yardstick wielding. Fortunately, John McInroe, Stan Musial, Mark Twain, or Boomer Esiason never encountered Sister Mary Pure. By the way, I have heard that it is now permissible for priests to date nuns, as long as they don't get into the habit. (Sorry about that, I just couldn't resist.)

My knuckles healed just fine (thanks to Father Steck), except for several remaining scars, and I never again was required to present my left hand for damage.

I am still left-handed, and no one ever swatted that sinister hand again. Whew.

CHAPTER 6

My Grandfather's Hearing Test

My grandfather, Albert F. Froussard, who got his thirtieth patent when he was eighty years old, was in his early nineties, and his hearing was almost gone. He had survived years earlier from a big bell-shaped object that fell off a large machine and crushed him against a truck. He was in a coma for three weeks, and when he came out of it, I was in the hospital room with him. He blinked his eyes several times and looked at me and said, "It's a damn good thing it happened to me, it would have killed anyone else."

That was my grandfather. He felt he was a super being with no flaws. However, he was fast approaching total deafness. This didn't appear to bother him as much as it totally aggravated his family and all who attempted conversation with him.

At his office when the phone would ring, he would answer the phone (he was quicker at that than anyone else in the office) and say at the top of his ninety-year-old lungs, "Hello. Hello . . . Hello . . . Who is this?" and "Speak up, we must have a bad connection."

My grandfather, since he was a highly successful inventor and businessman, felt he knew all, not unlike Al Capp's General

Bullmoose (what is good for General Bullmoose is good for the USA), my grandfather felt that he was pretty much an infallible being. He was not very receptive to suggestions from anyone. I am not saying that he was disliked at all, but his hearing deficiency was definitely disturbing to those around him. He had sixty-five machinists at one time or another and most had been with him for twenty years or more, and they respected him much; however, to put it as gently as possible, his hearing loss was driving everyone goofy! I worked in his drafting department, making catalogs and other miscellaneous tasks, every summer between semesters. I was going to come to the rescue and help my grandfather hear again.

I made an appointment with a hearing center on Hampton Avenue close to his home in St. Louis Hills. My grandfather and I always got along very well, so I convinced him that a hearing test would make his life much more enjoyable. He seemed to understand and agreed to let me take him there for a hearing exam. That was to be a wonderful event for my grandfather (and everyone else in his life), so I picked him up one Saturday morning for the exam I had scheduled.

We arrived in plenty of time. The audiologist was very friendly and highly complimentary to my grandfather, saying that he was amazed that he was in his nineties, but he certainly didn't look it. After all those pleasantries, he entered the booth (the cone of silence), and my granddaddy sat for the test. Well, it was determined after the test that his hearing was several degrees worse than Beethoven's, (well, actually at that time, it wasn't nearly as bad. Beethoven couldn't hear at all since he was dead), and the audiologist had the perfect hearing solution with a state-of-the-art hearing device for that time in the seventies. The hearing expert placed the hearing aids on my grandfather, and I could see from his facial expression that he could hear clearly for the first time in a decade or so. I had accomplished my goal, and the earth would be thrilled! Then the hammer dropped!

My grandfather said they were nice and asked how much they were. Bad question. As I remember, the audiologist told him around $500. My grandfather got up out of the chair, pointed his finger at the man, and screamed at the top of his lungs (I think the building actually shook), "YOU ARE A GODDAMN CROOK!"

My grandfather was serious. He was about six feet tall and considerably taller than the audiologist who looked at me with a very nervous expression and gently said, "Please take your grandfather away, and don't bring him back." I agreed and understood.

In the car taking him back home, he was still steaming from that hearing aid "crook" and said loudly, "If God wanted me to hear, he would let me hear."

I looked at his cane next to him on the seat and said to him, "Well, God wanted you to fall down, but you went against his wishes and bought a cane!" My grandfather looked at me and said even louder than he screamed at the hearing guy, "AW HELL!"

My grandfather passed away at 101 still not hearing.

CHAPTER 7

The Parkmoor Disaster

I had my daddy's 1956 orange and white Ford Victoria for a date with Joan and two other couples. We were all classmates at Bishop DuBourg High School and we were going to dinner and a movie. There was a St. Louis favorite drive in restaurant named The Parkmoor where the orange-jacketed carhops delivered the food. (Remember carhops?) They had great malts and burgers, and we were all hungry.

The carhop hopped to my car, and we all ordered our burgers, fries, sodas, and malts. The order was delivered to my side window on a tray with all of the burgers and fries, while the malts and sodas were delivered to Joan's door. Judy in the back seat decided that she had to go to the ladies' room, and she had to exit from the car by Joan's door that had all the drinks. The Ford Victoria was a two door, so Joan scooched even closer to me (nice) to allow the back of her seat to lean forward to allow Judy's egress. She climbed over Jim, and Dolores got out on Joan's side, then with the brains of a grape, she slammed the door. Yikes! All the water, soda, and malts left the tray with great speed and crashed all over the front and back seat carpet, girls, etc. Judy came back to the car seeing all of us out of the car and said, "What happened?" She had no idea of the disaster she caused.

All movie plans were cancelled and the dining experience was over. We could not let my dad know what we had done to his beautiful car. We went to J. C. Penny's and got cleaning supplies and towels to totally restore the beauty of the orange carpet, seats, girls dresses, and even the ceiling of the car. It was unbelievable the havoc and total mess that six drinks could cause.

I was worried that if traces of coke and malts were left in the car, it would be a very cold day in hell before my dad would let me use his car again, so the world-class restoration by the six of us spent hours restoring the interior and left no trace of the disaster we had caused. In truth, we were all such good friends and had such a great party cleaning the car, it was much more fun than any stinking movie would have been anyway.

While on the car subject, another story comes to mind. Roger Goessling was the oldest of our group of friends, and the only one that had his own car. Whenever we went anywhere, Roger drove. We would all chip in for gas, which, believe it or not, was around 20¢ a gallon.

"OK, guys, let's pay up," so we would all chip in a quarter or dime, so Roger could keep driving. I remember seeing a sign saying "Gas War. Carl Bolch regular .18 per gallon." Those really were the days. Roger's dad was some sort of muckety-muck with Railway Express Co. (a predecessor to UPS), and on one Saturday, Roger was going to work with his dad, leaving his car available for our cleaning the interior and washing the exterior as kind of a payback for his driving any time the group went somewhere. It was a great Saturday project.

Don Flaskamper, Ronnie Thoene, Dave Twist, and I thought it would be a great idea to go above and beyond Roger's expectations and cover the interior seats with a new cover, so we went to J. C. Penny's in Hampton Village to see what material was available. There before us on a rack was probably the most hideous leopard skin fabric we had ever seen. All the other fabrics seemed humdrum and unworthy for Roger's car. He just wanted us to clean his car, not reupholster it, but this seemed like a really fun and devilish prank to play on him, so we purchased what we felt would be a sufficient amount of cloth. It was on sale (I guess it had been there so long with no one wanting it), and I think we spent $8.00 at the most. This was not even a classy fabric (if leopard skin could ever be so), it really looked as cheap as it was.

So we drove Roger's car back to his house and commenced working on his surprise. We covered the front and back seats tightly using a staple's gun Dave's dad had, and it really looked just as hideous as we anticipated. We had plenty of material left, so we covered the overhead, the side armrests, and everywhere we could think of. There was a cover on the horn in the center of the steering wheel, and we popped off the metal casing and covered the horn button with leopard skin. We even covered the sun visors on both sides with that hideous material. Roger's '47 Chevy coupe looked totally ridiculous with all of those spots leaping out at you as soon as you opened the door. We finished the project and hung around, waiting for Roger to scream when he saw what we had done to his car. Roger's dad brought him home around 5:00, and we couldn't wait for his reaction.

However . . .

He loved it! He proudly possessed the silliest looking car on the planet, and I guess that our prank had an even happier ending. He kept it that way until the car let out its last roar and finally collapsed to big cat country.

CHAPTER 8

The Acolyte Aspirant

St. Joan of Arc church had finally completed constructing the elementary school that was only a block and a half from my home. It was a brand new school and I was excited to attend. I was only a half year from being able to serve mass. At that time, most good Catholic boys heading for fourth grade aspired for that occasion, as it was a major step in getting to be a grown-up. This was very similar to a Jewish boy's bar mitzvah. It was entering into the "Big Time!" I was confirmed at St. Gabriel's church by my savior from my left-handed persecution, Monsignor Steck. I was ready to enter the new school and eligible for serving mass, so finally I would get to wear the grown-up cassock and surplice. Big time! I was very religious at that time and seriously thought about becoming a priest later in life. That is until I learned about that celibacy thing.

I have been fortunate to have a very good and accurate memory. Sister Dolorene the third, fourth, fifth, and sixth grade teacher (she taught third and fourth grades, so I had her for two years; then she taught fifth and sixth grades, so two more years of Sister Dolorene). Sister Dolorene learned of my memory talent very quickly and used me for whatever benefit she determined. At the start of fourth grade, she presented me with the acolyte's manual, and I gobbled it up and had it memorized very quickly. She was impressed with my speed, pronunciation, and accuracy, and had me tutor the other eligible students in learning the responses to the priest during mass.

The procedures of the mass rituals were taught to us by the new parish priest, Father Rider. All of the mass proceedings were done in the church by the altar. We learned how to accompany Father when he was delivering the Holy Communion and, very importantly, how to present the cruets of the water and wine during the service. (Father Rider always consumed a complete vessel of the wine and just a dewdrop of water to make it truly holy).

Father Rider also had a great sense of humor and very little hair on his head, and told his future servers, "I have thirteen hairs on my balding head, I part them down the middle, and a major decision I have every morning is which side of my skull to put the odd one."

In the Roman Catholic mass, the acolyte gives the responses to the priest, which at that time were all in Latin. The mass was spoken in Latin, and for me, that made the church attendance a very special and sacred experience. Mass at that time was certainly different from ordinary life, and it made church attendance a very special occasion, even though we didn't know what in the hell the priest was saying. When the Catholic Church decided to change the Latin Mass to English and have the priest turn and face the congregation, it took away much of the mystique and splendor of the mass for me. I considered the priest a very special man and not just one of the congregation's buddies. I think that in order to draw more church members, they destroyed the special mystique of the Catholic mass. Nevertheless, at that time, the priest spoke in Latin, and the acolytes responses were in Latin as well. My responsibility was to assist the aspirants to learn the responses and prepare for mass assistance.

My first mass was being served at the 5:30 a.m. hour, a generally lightly attended service, and for rookie acolytes, usually their first mass. I, however, was no rookie. I had the responses in the palm of my hand. I was the acolyte tutor.

The performers (Father Rider and I) were in place and ready to start Holy Mass. The newbies first mass was usually at a very early time, so my debut was at the 5:30 a.m. mass. Father Rider and I exited the sacristy and took our respectful positions to start the Holy Mass, Father stood facing the altar, held his hands high toward the heavens and said, "In nomine Patris, et Filii, et Spiritus Sancti," and I was off and running for my assisting role.

I started by saying, "Ad deum qui laetificat, juventutem meam." I then said "quoniam ad hoc, blabber labber." I slightly paused again and said "mumble mumble deus something," all while the priest's hands were still extended heavenly.

He continued in that position and ready to speak while I continued my memorized responses. It appeared that every so often, his hand position took a momentary slight surge, as if to say something, but I kept giving my responses, flawlessly and with great speed. With his hands still extended, he lowered his head and quietly said to me, "Please wait for me." Egad, I was about a third of the way through the Mass when he was still on the opening salvo.

Fortunately, for the subsequent mass servings, I was much more gracious in allowing the priest to direct the proceedings.

— Chapter 9 —

Sister Bee and the Special Chorus

At Bishop DuBourg High School, there were close to two thousand students, and it was the brand new flagship school in the archdiocese. With so many students, there were many with outstanding voices. I was not possessed with an outstanding voice, although it was good enough for an elitist choral group called the Special Chorus. We performed in all of the school's productions, "Showboat," "Daddy Long Legs," "Song of Norway," and "Brigadoon." Great times were had.

The chorus director was a delightful nun named Sister Beatrice Marie, better known by all choral members as Sister Bee. Unlike most nuns, she was really attuned to the happenings of the day and was considered to be really with it. (As an example of the other nuns who weren't "with it," Elvis Presley was the biggest thing on the planet, and in the first day of second year Latin class, Sister Verona had us all write our names on a paper that was passed to her so she could learn who was who in our class. She would read the name on the sheet and ask that person to say a few words for identification. Someone [me] wrote the name Elvis Presley, and she read the name and said, "Elvis, Elvis, where are you?") Sister Bee wasn't like that at all, she knew all about Elvis, and also all the lyrics to Harry Belafonte's "Jamaica Farewell," and just about every new hit song. We were one big happy family. Our chorus was chosen to visit the other schools and perform, mostly due to several gifted sopranos, some very talented tenors, and one terrific bass who could very comfortably hit a low D and belt it out like Thurl Ravenscroft, (Mr. Grinch).

Sister Bee who was very up with current real life happenings always had some special thing for us to do together after rehearsals. She created a very close-knit group, and cemented lifelong relationships for years to come.

On Ash Wednesday, the first day of the forty-six days before Easter, Catholics are reminded of "Ashes to ashes and dust to dust" with a black cross of ashes on the forehead given by the priest at Mass, and all good Catholics are expected to do some sort of penance by "giving up for Lent" something. It always seemed to me that people sacrificed by giving up something they were trying to give up anyway, like smoking, eating fattening foods (trying to lose weight), or something more self-serving for improvement. At that time, meat on Friday during Lent was a definite no-no. Now it seems like the only time to forego meat is the actual Ash Wednesday.

On the morning of Ash Wednesday at the 7:00 a.m. Special Chorus rehearsal, Sister Bee asked several chorus members what they were giving up for Lent.

"Betty Bohr, what are you giving up for Lent?"

"Sister, I am giving up chocolate until Easter."

"Beverly Shea, what are you giving up?"

"I'm giving up ice cream, Sister, and I really love ice cream,"

"Audrey Georger, what are you giving up?"

"I'm giving up soda, Sister"

And so on, then she came to me. Sister Bee always called me by my last name and said, "Marquess, what are you giving up for Lent?'

I said, "Sister, I always felt that a true sacrifice was giving up something dearly loved, so for Lent, I am giving up the Catholic Church!" Sudden dead silence fell upon the room. Sister Bee just looked at me with no expression whatsoever, then her right foot started tapping slowly, and that great twinkle in her eye gave her away, and she started laughing, gathered herself together, and said "Say two Hail Mary's, One Our Father, take two aspirins, and call me in the morning." That was Sister Bee, very hard to have one on her!

CHAPTER 10

The Incredibly Powerful 1957 Mercury

My dad had an orange and white 1956 Ford Victoria that had orange carpeting, an orange padded dash, an orange steering wheel, and even orange sun visors. It was a very remarkable piece of machinery. It was time for my mom to get a new car, and she opted for a 1957 Mercury. She liked the orange and white of my dad's car and found an orange and white one on Trigg Mercury's showroom floor (Trigg will give you the shirt off his back). However, this one had very special package, which included a 290 horsepower engine. Why my mom wanted that car was a puzzlement to me because she rarely drove over thirty-five miles per hour. Cars behind were always honking at her to drive faster. It truly was much more of a car that she needed, but she liked it and it was hers. One weekend in 1958, she let me take it to Columbia, Missouri, where Roger Goessling and I were roommates at Missouri University. What an absolute thrill for me. That car had been deprived of a real workout and rarely hit 40mph.

From St. Louis on Highway 40 (now I-70), we headed to Columbia. There are several steep hills and I was just itching to see what that car could really do. So coming down one of those steep hills, I floored it. We were picking up speed very quickly, and that incredibly powerful engine was putting out all it was worth. The speedometer kept climbing, and hit 110 miles per hour. I became scared to death, so I slowed down as fast as I could. As we peaked the top of the hill, there was a highway patrol car with lights flashing, and the man with the pointed hat signaled me to pull over.

My roommate said, "You are toast, pal."

I started to pull over and was still at a faster speed than I should have been, and the highway patrol officer had to jump out of my way to avoid being knocked into the ditch. I knew I was doomed.

He approached the window and said to me as I was shivering and scared to death, "Do you know how fast you were going? Son, you were clocked at eighty-seven miles per hour."

I nervously said while the sweat began to pour, "Oh, thank God. This is my mom's car, we are just heading back to college for the weekend, and I wanted to see what this car with its mighty big engine would do, but when it hit 110, I got scared and slowed down."

My roommate let out some sound that resembled the cry of a banshee, while the officer just stared at me in disbelief. I think that I was just so nervous I couldn't think clearly, and the officer just continued to stare at me and started to laugh. I had presented my license, and he noticed that I was only seventeen (I probably looked like I was eight years old and got caught with my hand in the cookie jar) as he continued to stare at me while still laughing.

He said to me "Son, that is a new one for me, and this is my eighteenth year on the force, I never heard anyone say they were going faster than they were clocked, so slow down and enjoy the rest of the day."

I said "Thank you, officer, I will!" I rolled up the window as the adrenaline kicked in and I started really shaking! I didn't even receive a written warning, much less a speeding ticket. In that incident, honesty was indeed, the best policy!

CHAPTER 11

Berkshire Hathaway

In 1955, my brother's wife, Millie, worked for a stockbroker named John Heslop who was with a firm named Reinholt and Gardner. She was his administrative assistant and heard about many stocks, which she told my mom about. My mom and dad mostly invested in mutual funds, investments that had low risk and small profit potential, but were pretty safe investments. My mom had $1,000 to invest one day and Millie told her that Mr. Heslop liked two stocks, Berkshire Fine Spinning and Peabody Coal, which was a solid company established in 1883, the year my maternal grandfather was born. So my mom spent her $1,000 between those two companies. She bought ten shares of Berkshire and forty shares of Peabody. She told me at the time the Berkshire company made Hathaway shirts, and she bought that stock for me. I didn't think about it again until my breakfast buddy, Peter Marcus, a fine artist and professor at Washington University, told me about a conversation he had with friends the night before at dinner.

Peter said that the conversation had turned to stock investments and a stock named Berkshire Hathaway was $1,700 per share. What? Who ever heard of a stock priced that high?

I wondered if that had any connection to the Berkshire Fine Spinning stock my mom bought way back in the fifties. So the next day I called her and asked.

"That is the worst stock we have ever owned! It never paid a dividend, and it never split, it is a useless stock." (My parents only bought stocks for the interest and dividends.)

"But Mom, it is $1,700 a share!"

"I don't care, it never pays anything to its shareholders! You can have it, I bought it for you."

My, my, that sounded great to me. I said "Swell mom, do it."

By the time it was transferred weeks later, the stock hit around $2,600 per share. It was like the heavens opened and showered me with money. Whoever heard of a stock being $2,600 per share? The transfer was made, and I had those shares in my grubby paws! I got reports from the company for a while, and the stock hovered around $2,500 per share. My son Donny was invited to the National Music Camp in Interlochen, Michigan, and my son Danny was going to Camp Taum Sauk that summer. Piffle. I had the bucks if I cashed in my "useless" Berkshire stock. So I sold it for $2,500 per share—big bucks a share. I sat back and admired myself for my incredible brilliance!

Not so fast, Dumbo! That stock today as of this writing closed at $442,000 per share! I could buy Cleveland with that money (not really, but it would be a lot of cash).

As a realistic remark, I know for certain that I would not still have that stock today. I would have sold it long before it came anywhere close to a measly $300,000 per share.

As a side note, I had that stock being held in my account with A. G. Edwards in St. Louis, where I had also purchased a stock named Marinduque Mining at .01 per share. My stockbroker, Alan Hartman, said that I was not his largest customer, but certainly his most diverse!

CHAPTER 12

Dr. Dick

Richard London was my best friend as I was growing up (an achievement still in progress), and we both felt that the world was our play toy. We had much fun together and the world was our oyster.

We lived a block away from each other. One day, Dick and I were talking on the phone together, and Dick asked me to hold on a moment. A few minutes later, there was a knock at my back door while I was holding the phone waiting for Dick to come back on the line. I ran to the back door saw Dick there and said "Come in, I am on the phone," then I realized how dumb that was.

Months later, we were walking next to a phone booth at Hampton Village when the phone in the booth was ringing, I went to answer it, and there was no one on the phone. I pretended to talk for a moment and called out to Dick, "It's for you!" Dick walked to the booth, picked up the phone and realized that I got him back.

One very delightful evening, driving with all of the windows open in the car, we pulled up to a stop light and to our right was a car with two great looking girls with their windows open as well. I heard Dick yell at the top of his lungs something very obscene regarding those girls and how deliciously attractive they were. I turned and saw Dick scrunched on the floor below the window, and the only one visible to those girls was me. I received a glare from them thinking I was the person that said that horrible thing regarding them. Dick was hiding out of sight on the floor, laughing his vulgar head off! I was so embarrassed that those girls would think I said those really bad things. Even way back then, four-letter words were not part of my vocabulary. Dick knew it, and he loved embarrassing me so.

One of our favorite things to do when we entered Howard Johnson's or Steak and Shake, we would choose a booth next to a couple of really old ladies (probably fifty or so), and we would sit and start talking nonsense loud enough for them to eavesdrop and try to follow our conversation. The rules for our conversation were this: Neither one of us could say anything that had to do with what the other one of us was saying. Our conversations typically would be like this:

DICK: Is she feeling better now after the attack?

DON: I can't make it Saturday. Let's try for Sunday.

DICK: I have eaten there before and got really sick on that fish.

DON: I think political science or Asian tropical diseases.

DICK: It is now showing at the Esquire Theater. I would love to see it.

DON: Yes, that is right. She should never wear that again. Those colors just don't work together.

DICK: I've got $12 dollars, maybe that is enough

DON: I think he has some burr or something in his right front paw.

And so on and on.

We felt it was so much fun putting them in a situation of trying to figure what the hell we were talking about.

We also created a vocabulary of great words that to date have no meaning. Wonderful sounding words that have no definition. We created these great words that eventually will certainly be given meaning, they are just too wonderful to have no assignation.

Words: Snargel, Zorch, Twimbel, Thobblewakky, and the finest word ever, Urbrumpoo!

We felt then, as I do now, those words are just too wonderful to have no meaning. Dr. Dick and I are still hoping!

Dick continued on with his life and became a noted psychologist in helping patients overcome their summer crazies. (Totally disregarding his own as well as mine.)

CHAPTER 13

Naja Karamaru

There was a burlesque theater in St. Louis called the Grand, where they had old burlesque comedians and skits plus four or five exotic dancers (strippers), including a top star. Our group saw that a headliner named Naja Karamaru was going to appear. We knew nothing about Naja, but the teaser photo in the *Post-Dispatch* looked like she was gorgeous. The four of us, Roger Goessling, 6'5"; Gary Duecker, 6'7"; Larry Giesing, 6'2"; and me, 6'1", thought it would be fun for us to attend the show. In truth, none of us had been there before. We had a smart ass plan, which was for us to purchase several newspapers, sit in the front row, watch the comedians, and laugh at their age old and tired jokes and skits. Then when the strippers came out, we would ignore them and read the papers until their act was over, put the newspapers down, watch the comedians, then continue reading the newspapers when the next stripper came out. It was just a plan made by smart alec teenagers, but we thought it would be really funny (at least to us).

I know that was a dumb and insulting thing for us to do to the dancers (strippers); however, this prank was not my idea. Nevertheless, all of us were very willing to participate and thought it would be great fun. It was a devilish prank, and the four of us, being well over six feet and taking up four seats directly in the front row, were certainly obvious to the others in the theater. We may have been the only ones enjoying our prank, but we certainly thought it was funny.

Then the emcee announced the headline exotic dancer (stripper), Naja Karamaru. Wow! She came on stage, and one by one, we slowly dropped our newspapers and just stared and lusted after Naja. She was built like she was drawn by Al Capp (Lil' Abner's Daisy Mae, or Moonbeam McSwine) and possessed a drop-dead gorgeous smile, and she kept looking directly at us. She was also a great dancer and extremely adept with classic and very beautiful movements. As her act continued and her clothes dropped, she proved that she was indeed an incredible feminine specimen. This was 1958, and we had never seen such a beautiful lady. It didn't matter to us that at the end of her act, she still was a lady and remained partially clothed. We fell in love anyway. Her act ended too soon, but we all were very happy that we saw her. Burlesque was not what we thought.

There was a hotel directly connected to the Grand called the York Hotel, and we assumed that it was where the dancers were being housed. We really wanted to meet Naja. It was decided that I would be a Brazilian who spoke no English but was a close friend of Naja's, and I was just visiting St. Louis and saw that she was appearing there. So the four of us entered the hotel lobby and walked up to the front desk. I said some gibberish to my friends that I felt sounded Spanish, and Gary Duecker interpreted to the desk clerk that I spoke no English and was a very close friend of my aunt Naja. I continued blabbering in Spanglish with no meaning to any of my created words when the desk clerk turned to me and, in perfect Spanish, started speaking to me. I was at a total loss as what to say, and he continued speaking directly to me in Spanish (at least it certainly sounded like real Spanish, but it may have just been a higher form of gibberish), so I looked at my three friends, said my gibberish, turned, and headed for the door. They followed with great speed and the jig was up. However, it was a fun afternoon no less!

— CHAPTER 14 —

April McIntire

During my photography career, I purchased my film and photographic paper supplies from either Schiller's Camera (the one most professional photographers frequented) and Creve Coeur Camera, which catered to both hopeful amateurs and pros. Joe Crabtree was the sales person that I usually dealt with. One day, I came in and next to Joe at the counter was a very attractive lady. She was tall and cleverly constructed with long brunette hair, beautiful brown eyes, and a delightful smile. I just had to meet her. I was very happily married to my beautiful wife, Susan, and never strayed, and had no intention of doing so; however, I just had to have Joe's new assistant wait on me. Joe could tell that I (like every red-blooded male in the store) wanted to meet her. Her name was April McIntire.

I picked up a package of professional photo wipes, brought it up to the counter and asked her if she could help me.

"Good morning, ma'am, I am frustrated. All I can find are these professional photo wipes, where are your amateur photo wipes?"

She looked very puzzled. Joe Crabtree standing behind her was silently laughing, and she said to me, "I don't think there is such a thing as amateur photo wipes. What is wrong with these?"

"Well," I replied, "I am not a professional and really shouldn't try to use these . . . I don't know how, I would probably make many mistakes."

Joe interrupted the exchange and said, "April, meet Don Marquess, he is just pulling your leg." (Didn't I wish.)

April had a very delightful sense of humor in addition to being a very attractive lady, so she became my sales person whenever I went to Creve Coeur Camera. April was a photographer as well and offered to mount my portfolio prints, as she was quite good at doing so. I used April as the hostess for several of my gallery shows, and people seemed to like her as much as my photos. (Later I referred to my photos as "images" rather than "photos." My good friend Lewis Portnoy, Hall of Fame photographer, told me I could charge more if I called them images.) April and I became good friends, and she mounted the prints I made for five or six of my portfolios. We had a very fun working relationship. Susan met her and thought she was a delight.

One afternoon, as I approached her at the counter, she met me with a great smile and said, "Don, I finished my portfolio, would you like to see it?"

April was a very beautiful lady who was an aspiring photographer, so I welcomed the opportunity and was anxious to see her work. She reached under the counter and brought out a very nice black portfolio album, opened it to the first black and white photo, and there standing next to a tree in a heavily wooded area was April . . . *totally naked*!. Yikes! I was speechless and totally dumbfounded. I had wondered for a long, long time just what was hidden under her clothes, and here in beautiful black and white was her naked body with those beautiful brown eyes looking directly at the camera. I couldn't believe it. I had no Idea what to say. I probably said nothing while trying to keep from stuttering.

I had a very good friend, an architect, Bob Entzeroth, who was a Fellow in the AIA, and when we were having lunch one afternoon at his St. Louis Club, I related my April McIntire story. I said, "Bob, I thought about her great body for years, and I guess like every guy I knew, I desired to see it unclothed. When it was there staring at me in glorious black and white, I became embarrassed and didn't know what to say."

Bob just looked at me with his devilish eyes and said, "There was only one thing to say . . . nice tits, babe!" (That was Bob, always knowing just the right thing to say at just the right time.)

Chapter 15

The True Definition of Art

The Saturday morning breakfast group that I was invited to join in 1982 still exists today, although there has been many changes in members in the last forty-one years. Some moved, some passed away, and new breakfasters joining. When it started, it was with a group of professional photographers. Lew Portnoy (Hockey Hall of Fame: Photographer's Wing), Chuck Dresner (St. Louis Zoo's official photographer), Bob Bishop (Stanford University, Ansel Adams Workshops, and Purina Cat Calendar), Neil Sauer (Anheuser Busch photographer, top photo studio in the Midwest), and Herb Wightman (director of photographic services at Washington University and St. Louis Football Cardinals's photographer)—a prestigious group indeed. I was invited because of my Great Forest Park Balloon Race art photos and the recent success I had with those photos. The breakfasts were a great relief to business and deep and serious personal issues were definitely verboten. In later years, we invited the noted psychiatrist, David Berland, to keep us on the straight and narrow. Recently we invited the retired exhibits director for the St. Louis Art Museum and an excellent landscape photographer, Dan Esarey.

Herb Wightman, Lou Portnoy, and I attended a two-day seminar at Missouri Botanical Gardens by noted photographer, Ernst Haas, a world famous photographer who excelled in black and white as well as color photography. A rarity in the photographic world to excel in both. The seminar was indeed educational and greatly enjoyable, as Ernst had a highly sophisticated sense of humor as well as a very insightful approach to photography.

After the second seminar, Ernst was approached by Herb Wightman, who had a photo to show Ernst and get his opinion. He showed the photo to Ernst, who looked at it and passed it back to Herb. Herb passed it back to Ernst, wanting him to look at it deeper, and immediately passed it back to Herb.

He said to Herb, "This photo is photojournalism, not art. It carried a message. I got it, and that is all I need to know. Art is determined by how long you want to look at it. I got the message, and that is all. You made your statement, and I got it, but it is not art." (If Ernst would have said that to me, I would have jumped out the window and sobbed while being pelted by the freezing rain.)

That statement of "Art is determined by how long you want to look at it" is the most descriptive statement possible that there could be regarding art. It applies to photos, paintings, drawings, music (how long you want to listen to it) automobiles, and beautiful women. If something about that piece of art compels you to look at it again and again, or to listen to it over and over, it is truly art. It applies to all classic pieces of anything that has endured the test of time!

CHAPTER 16

Liar's Poker

The Saturday morning Breakfast Club originally consisted of many very successful photographers. Most photographers, or anyone in the public eye, have an ego. Actors, artists, vocalists, musicians, anyone who puts his talent on display has an ego for sure. The great Spencer Tracy said, "Acting is a great profession, but don't let anyone catch you doing it!" The appearance of humility, whether feeling it or not, is a necessity in life. One of our breakfast members had an ego off the charts, and exhibited it with remarkable regularity. He was a great golf photographer, and did extensive photographic assignments for major Fortune 500 companies. He always made a big point of letting us know of his "greatness." Out of respect for the photographic profession and my fear of being sued, he will remain nameless.

One Saturday morning when the breakfast check arrived, on one of the very rare times that I had a hundred dollar bill in my possession (which remains true today). I stated with a very boastful way as I produced my hundred dollar bill, "This is the smallest I have, does anyone have change?"

I thought that was very funny, as did the other breakfast guys, except one. The egotist pulled out a hundred dollar bill and said, "Do you want to play Liar's Poker with our hundreds?"

I thought he was joking and said, "Sure. How do you play Liar's Poker?"

He explained that it is played with the serial numbers on the bill. Without showing the bill, you state how many matching serial numbers are on the bill. Two 2s is a pair, consecutive 5 numbers is a straight, three of anything is three of a kind, three of one number and two of another is a full house, and etc. My serial number had four 4s.

I said, "One pair." He believed me.

He said, "Two pairs." I believed him.

I said, "Three of a kind." He didn't believe me. I showed him my bill with four 4s and gleefully took his hundred. That dirty, lousy bum pulled out his money clip and fanned out twelve hundred dollar bills, just to show me how pitiful and insignificant my lousy one hundred dollar bill was.

So I invited two of my friends and their wives, along with Susan, to go to dinner with me at the China Garden. After dinner, we all got in the car and called Mr. Egotist, and thanked him in unison for the fine meal he provided!

CHAPTER 17

Really Good ... Then Really Bad

My entertainment career spanned for five to six years or so, and the original professional career included a trio in which a talented guitarist, John James, who had a beautiful tenor voice, but a total inability to harmonize, was the lead vocal. The building could fall down around the trio, and we knew that John's unfailing melody would survive. Years later, after my many involvements in other vocal ensembles, John was performing as a solo at a Ramada Inn in north St. Louis County. Susan and I went to hear him. His voice was still a beautiful unwavering tenor, and as a solo performer, he had no harmonizing challenges. After his first set, he came to our table to chat.

After the usual pleasantries were exchanged, he said, "I bought a gun today, and I am going home to murder my wife!"

What?

Susan and I thought he was kidding, but after a few moments, we realized that he was dead (sorry) serious. He said that he found a letter from a visitor to his neighbor's house the week before, thanking his wife, Evelyn, in detail for the great sex he had with her the week before. John said he was going to go home, wake his daughter, confront his wife, and then kill her after letting his daughter know how bad her mom had been. He was serious!

I said, "John, for god's sake, don't do it, you will spend the rest of your life in prison or, worst, get the electric chair. Listen to me and do it this way. First of all, get rid of the gun. Take it back, or throw it in the bushes somewhere. Now, go home, discover the letter, and after reading it, become enraged. Go to the kitchen, grab a sharp knife, and stab your wife many times, drop the knife, and stand there stupefied for a few moments, then go to the phone and call the police and say—now this is very important John. Use these exact words and say to the police—'I think I just killed my wife.' Temporary insanity, John, that is your defense."

Both John and my wife, Susan stared at me slack-jawed. John looked at me and finally laughed and said, "Wow . . . you are just as crazy as I am!"

After his second set, Susan and I headed home, and she praised me for my brilliance in painting such a ridiculous picture for John so he would realize his stupidity. She said "Don, that was perfect, you knew just what to say to jar his mind. The two of you have been friends for so long that he realized how dumb his murderous plan was and you beautifully pointed it out to him. Bravo."

Then when we were halfway home, Susan said, "What if he does it just the way you told him?"

Yikes! We had a very uncomfortable silence for several moments after that. Then the glee and glorious praise for my suggestion turned quickly to trepidatious fright. What if he does it? Those words kept repeating over and over in my mind. The rest of the ride home was greatly horrific, wondering if he really would do it. It plagued our thoughts all night, and most of the next day.

I picked up Susan after work, and we both felt that just a casual drop by to John's house was in order. We drove over. Before knocking on the door, we looked through the back window at the kitchen and saw a dozen or so long-stemmed roses thrown on the floor, and the huge refrigerator face down on the kitchen floor. We knocked on the door, and John's wife, Evelyn, opened the door for us. Her eyes were puffy red, as she had obviously been crying for a while, and said to us "The marriage is over, and John just can't accept it."

John then came into the kitchen and said to us, "Thanks for checking on us, I am OK now."

John's next several marriages were not quite as colorful.

CHAPTER 18

We Hit the Big Time

In the early sixties, folk music was really a big thing with the Kingston Trio, the Limeliters, Peter, Paul, and Mary, and about four million other folk groups forming everywhere. I was in a trio of two very fine musicians, of which I was not one. I was a French horn and trumpet player, not a guitarist. Fortunately, it wasn't required because the other two guys in the group were accomplished musicians on the guitar and banjo. I handled the microphone introductions and hopefully the humor in the group. Many people said that I sounded just like Bob Shane in the Kingston Trio. I readily admit it was a conscious effort, but I guess I did sound like him.

Gaslight Square in St. Louis was an entertainment center much like Bourbon Street in New Orleans, and on any given night in the summer, there were very large crowds walking the street and entering one of the thirty-plus clubs and restaurants on this three-block section of St. Louis at the juncture of Boyle and Olive. We played at many of the clubs, including the Laughing Buddha coffee club, the Tiger's Den, and the Crystal Palace. The Smother's Brothers, Barbara Streisand (at the beginning of her career), Miles Davis, Woody Allen, and others performed at the Crystal Palace periodically.

We ended up at Jack's or Better for the better part of three years. Every club was packed each night, and Jack's was no exception. Jack was a brilliant club owner. Our first nightly show was at 9:00 p.m. There would be a crowd waiting to get in. Jack had all of the lights on high and charged a cover charge of five bucks a head with a two drink minimum. He would fill the club, turn down the lights, and introduce the Town Criers (us). We would do a twenty-five-minute show, then leave the stage with the customers clapping.

Jack would say, "Let's bring 'em back." We came back, as pre-programmed, and did a twenty-minute or so encore, and then we would leave the stage. Jack would then turn the bright lights on again and clear the house for the next group waiting to come in. He would say as the house was clearing, "The Town Criers will be back at 9:00 p.m. tomorrow night." He would then let the next group in, and we would do another twenty-five-minute show, and Jack would play the same game, fill the house, and take their money. He would then graciously invite them back for the next night's performance. He didn't want any stragglers hanging around for the next show. He wanted those new cover charges.

Our last show was at midnight and there was always another throng waiting to get in. We were not great, but we were good enough, and everyone seemed to leave satisfyingly entertained. For all of the money that Jack turned six nights a week, on Saturday night, he paid us $360 to split with the three of us. Jack took in twice that amount with just one of our three nightly sets. But we were happy to receive the money for having a hell of a lot of fun and feeling like big stars.

Chapter 19

The Presidential Suite

With the enormous success of folk music in the sixties, and our years on Gaslight Square, the largest hotel in St. Louis, the Chase Park Plaza wanted to cash in on the Folk Fad, so we were stolen from our Gaslight Square home of Jack's or Better and lured with a $650 a week salary. We jumped at the opportunity for fame and double fortune and went west to the big time Chase Hotel. That venue was highly respected by the press and a full-page article by Dickson Terry was written in the *Post-Dispatch*. All systems were ready for us to perform in the Steeplechase room. We were having lots and lots of fun singing in the top hotel in St. Louis, and with the press influence of the Chase, our reviews were terrific.

I have been a major Cardinals fan since I was eight years old and loved the Cardinals with every fiber of my being. In September of 1963, the Dodgers were playing a series in St. Louis and staying at the Chase. They all came to the Steeplechase room that evening where we were performing, and I was somewhat rude to them. The Cardinals were in a pennant race, and the Dodgers were strong contenders as well. That day, the Dodgers beat the Cardinals in a day game, and

I was not happy with their arrival. Being such a huge fan, I was suffering from that loss and just couldn't contain my emotion, although the friendly jabs back and forth made for a very exciting performance. I feel it was our best show ever.

There was a late night open cafe in the Chase named the Tack Room, and we all had a late night snack together and they were very friendly and gracious to our trio. Sandy Koufax and Don Drysdale were especially nice to us. Leo Durocher not so much, but it was a fun late night event for us anyway. Afterward, at 2:30 a.m. or so, we went to the dressing room to collect our coats, store our instruments, and head home.

Not so fast. Our key didn't open the dressing room. This was not good at all since our car keys, and other possessions were locked in the room. We went to the front desk, and the night manager said that earlier someone had broken in the room and took several of the items that the Mary Kaye Trio, who were performing in the big room, the Chase Club, so they had the locks changed. The manager said that we were supposed to have been delivered the new key, but apparently, we didn't notice the delivery, so we went back to the Steeplechase room. No envelope and no key! We were at a major loss and couldn't even get into our cars to head home. It was after 3:00 a.m., and we had no place to go. The hotel was sold out, no rooms, except one.

The night manager said, "How would you, guys, like a nice treat? The Presidential Suite is unoccupied for this evening, and you gentlemen can have it!"

We didn't have to think very long and jumped at the offer.

We entered the suite, and ye gods, what a suite! It had three bedrooms, a living room, a dining room, four bathrooms, and a two-story window with a great view of the city. We called our wives and woke them up to explain that we were spending the night in very plush accommodations. If my memory serves correctly, we didn't sleep at all, and just worked on some new songs and had a great time doing so. The acoustics were just great. Around 9:00 a.m., we went downstairs to get the new key from housekeeping and had a very difficult time deciding to return the Presidential Suite key, but reluctantly gave it back. I requested another dressing room lock change so we could spent the next night there, but the morning clerk said that room was available again for that night if we wished to pay $925. We declined the offer, but that suite alone was enough of an incentive to run for president. None of us did, however.

CHAPTER 20

Susan's Delightful Grandmother

Susan and I had been married for several years, and I had met her parents, her aunt, and her uncle; but I never met her grandmother, Mary Miller. Mary Miller came to St. Louis to visit for a week or so, and she and I got along very well. I gave her a day-long tour of my beloved St. Louis and impressed her greatly. I am very proud of this city and love to show people how great it is. Susan's grandmother lived in Woodbury, New Jersey, just North of Philadelphia and very close to New York City, so impressing her with the wonders of St. Louis was indeed a challenge. Mission accomplished. The tour ended with a concrete at Ted Drewes Frozen Custard (try to match that NYC).

We arrived at Susan's Uncle Burr's house after the tour, where we had a very scrumptious meal prepared by Burr's wife, Carolyn. It was a terrific day. After dinner, Susan's grandmother, Mary Miller, proceeded to relate her family history. She had an ancestry that was traced all the way back to the 1200s. She delighted in telling me how this man from Ireland married this lady from England, and how this Scotsman married this Londoner and so on. It seemed to be an endless story that delighted her in telling. I was very interested, but kept getting confused as to who married whom and when, and all of the names bombarded.

After this long dissertation, she looked at me with her sparkling and proudly dancing eyes and said, "And not one Catholic in the bunch!"

Well, well . . . I was baptized Catholic, had sixteen years of Catholic education, and actually considered becoming a priest at one time in my life. I certainly ruined the legacy and purity of her waspishness. I considered momentarily telling her, "Whoops, I just tainted your legacy." I just couldn't let her know how I fouled up her entire family. So I just said, "Gee, that is wonderful!" She seemed to agree, and we continued our friendly relationship as I drove her to the airport for departure.

When I told Susan about her grandma's boasting, she told me that she was so glad that I didn't reveal my Catholicism as Susan would have been ostracized for messing up the family purity.

Chapter 21

Ten Las Vegas Casinos in One Afternoon

Susan and I had been married for just a few months and were "goofy in love" (Susan's terminology, but I agreed), and we were dining at a sidewalk café in the Central West End of St. Louis. Susan likened that area to Greenwich Village in New York. It was a beautiful early spring day with cerulean blue skies and an unseasonably warm breeze. We were awaiting our lunch sandwiches and just enjoying each other's company. Susan was telling me something about her sister in San Francisco when a very attractive young lady was passing by on the sidewalk next to our table. She had a beautiful face and a very delightful and somewhat bouncy walk directly in front of our table. She captured my eye, and I stopped paying attention to what Susan was saying.

Susan noticed my admiring eyes, stopped the sister story, and said, "You think she is pretty good looking, don't you?"

Yikes, I was caught! In a very fortunate moment of quick thinking, I replied, "Susan, if I didn't like beautiful women, I never would have married you."

There was a very long silence as Susan just stared at me, and stared at me a little longer, then said "Oh . . . you are really good!"

I think that must have been the most fortunate statement of our marriage because she became my spotter of beautiful women and always pointed out one of special note, knowing that I knew that she herself, in my eyes, was the most attractive of all.

Two weeks later, we left for a trip to Las Vegas, one of the greatest cities on the planet. No other place has a totally different resemblance to anything in real life like Las Vegas. You will never find a clock in Las Vegas. Three or four days in Las Vegas is truly like being on a different earth, and it is an extreme departure from the daily existence in any other city in the US. We checked into the Castaways Resort and Casino, which was directly across Las Vegas Boulevard from the Sands. Both casinos are gone now and replaced by the Mirage and the Venetian. Susan loved the swimming pool at the Castaways; however, she forgot her swimming suit, which was just fine with me. She felt it was a necessity for sunning the poolside. I remembered seeing an ad or a movie short of a shop called Fredericks of Hollywood located in Las Vegas, so I suggested that we take a cab and head there. (I guess at that time, the only thing separating me from being a dirty old man was age. I have finally caught up.) Susan, in addition to being a strikingly beautiful lady, was very cleverly constructed, and it was very enjoyable seeing her modeling the various swimsuits and bikinis. She finally chose the least revealing and most tasteful swim attire in the store, but still whoop-de-doo as far as I was concerned. We headed back to the Castaways for her afternoon by the pool. I had a time-killing and fun expedition in mind.

I do not play slot machines as a general rule and feel that the term *one arm bandit* is aptly named. I think that most people who play slot machines go for the big money jackpots and usually play until all of the money is gone in their quest for jackpots. My mission was to prove that at one point in playing the slots, there would be a profit of some sort that was usually ignored with the quest for greater rewards. So my journey while Susan was sunning her beautiful self poolside began my slot adventure.

I decided to visit ten casinos and prove, at least to me, that my theory was correct. I would visit each of the ten casinos, go to the cashier, and purchase $10 in nickels. That was two hndred pulls on the *one arm bandit*. I wouldn't touch the nickels that made that hollow tin sound landing in the bucket, and would just play until the two hundred nickels were gone. I would then empty the trough, take the nickels to the cashier, and collect my total. It was a very fun way to spend an afternoon. I walked out of eight of those casinos with a profit ranging from $1.35 in one casino to a profit of $32.05 in a different one, with the other six being somewhere in between, resulting in an afternoon gain of just under $100. Neither casino of the two losing ones lost more than $5.00. My theory was proven, to me at least. Apparently, all of the casinos in the world learned of my proven theory, so now no more clang of nickels, dimes, and quarters echoing in the tin bowl. It is all paper now. No buckets, no blackened fingers, and no paper rolls of coins. Such a sad passing.

I returned to poolside to find my freshly roasted Susan napping in the recliner, wearing her sunglasses with a paperback book resting on her exposed tummy. I awakened her to brag about my proven theory, and she said "Great! Just don't let the casinos know, they will alter the payouts!"

We dined that evening at my favorite restaurant, the Ah, So Steak House, and for weeks later, the corner of the book imprint remained on her beautiful middle torso.

CHAPTER 22

Pardon Me, What Did You Just Say?

For years, it was a very welcome treat for a Cardinals game to be televised. Every game was broadcast on KMOX radio in St. Louis with 147 radio affiliates throughout the country. Before the Dodgers left Brooklyn in 1957, the St. Louis Cardinals were the furthest west baseball team and the furthest south baseball team. Most southern and western states considered the Cardinals to be their team of choice, so the Cardinals Baseball Network was one of the largest in the country. It remains the largest radio network in the MLB to this day. However, in 1981, games were telecast selectively, not every game was telecast. It was a fine event when a game was televised, with maybe a game per series being aired.

The games were, at one time, being televised on the NBC affiliate, KSDK with various personalities at the mike. On a particular game in 1982, Ron Jacober and Jay Randolph were handling color and play-by-play in a game against the Cincinnati Reds. In the fourth inning, the Cardinals were losing 4-0, and the Reds had runners on first and second with only one out.

Jay Randolph said on the air, "Doug Bair is throwing up in the bull pen."

After a long pause, Ron Jacober says, "Doug Bair is doing *what* in the bullpen?"

Jay Randolph, while laughing, says, "Doug Bair is throwing . . . up in the bull pen."

Ron Jacober said, "That didn't fix it, Jay."

Jay Randolph, who was a fine announcer for golf, and a superb gentleman that knew baseball very well, was still laughing when he rephrased his guffaw by saying, "Doug Bair is up and throwing in the bull pen."

To which Ron Jacober replied, "OK, Jay, I'll accept that!"

There is a very famous outrageous blunder with Harry Caray and Jack Buck during a

Cubs game at Wrigley Field that I wrote about in the first "Quickies" book that I advise you to read. Well, I guess that is an unfair plug for my first book, so I will just tell it again in this one.

It was a teen night event at Wrigley with a band to be playing after the game for dancing in the aisles and on the field. During the broadcast, both Harry and Jack noticed a teen couple paying far more attention to each other than the game, with hugging and kissing overshadowing their attention to game on the field. Jack and Harry mentioned this on the air several times.

After a while during the game Harry Caray says to Jack Buck, "Jack, I have been watching that teen couple in the stands, and he kisses her on the strikes, and she kisses him on the balls."

Jack just looked at Harry in total disbelief as to what Harry just said. Harry then realized his blunder and was laughing so hard. He pointed to Jack as if to say "save me." Jack then pointed back to Harry because he was laughing so hard he couldn't take over the mike. They broke in the middle of the inning for a commercial, then came back to the broadcast, but neither could speak again while still breaking up over the outrageous guffaw.

They broke again for a commercial, and after missing an entire inning, Jack took the mike and said to Harry "Let's just talk about the game being played on the field."

Harry's response was "Deal"

— Chapter 23 —

That is Not Exactly What I Meant, Ted

I am a readily admitted Ice Cream addict. I love it! Over the years, I have developed a somewhat snobbish attitude toward the richness in ice cream, the greater content of butterfat, the better for me. Just as a sort of tutorial regarding butterfat content, ice cream does not deserve the "ice cream" name until the butterfat content is 10 percent or greater. But that is not the entire story.

Air plays a big part in the final product. There is a devil called Over Run. Let's say that you start off with 100 oz. of your ice cream mix that is 10 percent butterfat, and you whip it up to give you 200 oz. of product, that is termed 100 percent overrun. So what you are tasting is 50 percent air. That makes the ice cream not taste nearly as great to me. I want the real stuff, not mostly air! It is a simple fact that air is free, and the more you can put in ice cream, the greater the yield. So in my ice cream, I always buy the more costly product. I don't like buying air. Haagen Dazs ice cream seems to have the least airy product and contains 16 percent to 18 percent butterfat, which is to my liking.

Another type of ice cream is Frozen Custard, which in addition to cream, milk, and sugar, it also contains egg yolks, making it smoother and more like the French variety of ice cream. It is served soft and smooth and delicious. There is a frozen custard stand in St. Louis called Ted Drewes Frozen Custard, which several years ago was termed the best ice cream in the world, an award that was given by a company in Ireland. Ted himself was given that trophy that is now proudly on display in his ice cream stand in St. Louis. Ted Drewes primary ingredients are cream, honey and eggs, which makes a delightfully delicious concoction that is hard for me to resist. His frozen custard has very little overrun, which makes an unbelievable and very smooth product that delights my pallet with the creamy deliciousness I love.

Ted Senior opened his first custard in Florida in 1929. The following year, he opened his first stand in St. Louis. In 1941, he opened his stand on Chippewa Street, very close to my boyhood home, the year after I was born. In the later forties, I used to ride my bike to his stand to get a cone of that delicious ice cream. Ted Junior has carried on the tradition of creating

---

that scrumptious ice cream with very few improvements since I traveled there in my childhood. Ted and I became friends since I was such a loyal and continual customer.

As an aside to this story, I remember that in the early fifties with Dairy Queen's national expansion that made a very different product (masquerading as ice cream) with the "curl on top," Ted's father was encouraged to try his hand in offering a similar product that had only 5 percent butterfat and mostly air like Dairy Queen's. He was his own worst enemy with that product that he named (if I remember correctly) Freezo. When a customer came to the window, he would say, "Do you want the real custard or that junk over there?" Freezo was very short lived.

Ted Drewes frozen custard became so popular that in 1985, he expanded his custard stand from five windows to twelve. Nowadays, if you pass his stand during his open hours, the lines leading to the street are about twelve people deep with most of the windows serving the customers so quickly that your wait for the creamy product may be no more than ten minutes or so. Ted is a major Cardinals fan, and since my closest friend for years was Marty Hendin, vice president of the Cardinals, Ted would always come out to talk baseball with me and to see if I had any inside information to impart.

On one particular June night, when all of the windows were packed and customers lined all the way out to the street, while talking to Ted, I said, "Ted, this is the first time I have ever seen a manual cash register overheat. I bet the only problem you have now is counting your money."

Ted said, "You know, you are right, wait here and I will show you something."

I waited and shortly Ted returned with a hand full of quarters. He lined them up in his hand, counted them by fours and in a flash said. "There. Ten dollars! People used to pay with quarters. They are easy and quick to count. Now people pay with dollar bills and higher, we have to flatten them all out, sort the $5s, $10s, and $20s, turn them the right way and band them in stacks for the bank. We stay an extra hour every night just counting the money!"

I almost said, "Ted, your story truly touched my heart," but I didn't. Instead, I said "That is not exactly what I meant, but I see the problem!"

— CHAPTER 24 —

My Jaguar XKE

My very good friends, Lon Gilbert and Barry Oxenhandler, were two of the finest musicians I have ever met. We sang together for a couple of years, performing on the entertainment area called Gaslight Square in St. Louis, and we remained close friends thereafter. Barry, an incredible natural musician, became the chief pilot for Enterprise Leasing. Lon, a studied musician, continued in the music business, playing guitar for Jerry Gotler's (a Juliard grad) band called the Chasers. Jerry Gotler was an outstanding clarinetist. Lon's brother, George, was in the group as well, and other than music, we all shared a love for poker.

The Chasers were in town one weekend, so I invited them to our apartment for a poker game. Low stakes of course, and the most you could bet was one dollar. There were a lot of 25¢ chips being bet if two people had good hands. It was always dealer's choice, and when the deck got to me, I always dealt 5 card stud. One down, four up. I guess I always felt it was the best game. This was long before Texas hold 'em became so popular. Other games that we played were five card draw and seven card stud. Never any cards wild, we thought wild card games were for kids or novices. We all understood the game and loved playing. Most of the time, when we played, the big winner of the night would win around $100 with the biggest loser losing maybe $30 or so. They were very fun games. However, evil lurked.

This night when the band came to my apartment, a silly game called guts came on the scene. It was more or less a complete gambling game with little or no skill involved. It was a game played against an imaginary player called the pot. Players got three cards face down and after looking at their cards, declare "in" or "out" as to whether they can beat the pot hand or not. Three dummy cards are placed in the center of the table face down, that becoming the hand to beat. If after looking at a player's hand, he declares "in," meaning that he thinks he can beat the pot hand. If other players declare "in," then the players that stay must beat the dummy hand. If they don't, they have to match the pot. All this action takes place before the "blind hand" is revealed. If one player beats the dummy cards in the pot, and the other players don't. Each player must match the pot and the winning player wins it all. However, if no one has a better hand than the dummy, each player who declared "in" must match the pot. A simple inexpensive poker game that can very quickly get out of control. That evening it got way out of control.

My friend Lon had to match the pot a couple of times and asked to borrow chips from me after he ran out of his own. The pot on this night grew to $80. Lon had to match the pot. and I loaned him $65 from my winning stack. That was lots of money to me. The pot grew with several more losing hands by several other players, and Lon again filled out an IOU to me for $630. Ridiculous for our little $1.00 limit poker game. Believe it or not, that pot continued to grow, and it was in the $1,000 range. Lon had to match and asked for another loan. I refused.

I said, "What do you have for collateral?"

He jokingly replied, "All I have tonight is my Jaguar XKE."
I said, "OK, I'll take it."

He gave me the keys to his XKE. I loaned the chips to match the pot to him. He matched the pot. This fun evening turned sour very quickly with this stupid game, but I had his Jaguar, and the evening continued. The pot got to be absolutely stupid, as it continued to grow beyond any sensible number. It got to a point where I had to match the pot, so I threw in Lon's keys to his Jaguar. My good friend Lon turned white as a sheet, and for a moment, I felt he would pass out. Something had to be done to stop this foolishness, so we all decided to end the game and split the pot equally. I grabbed Lon's keys and said, "I've got my share, you guys split the rest."

I was kidding of course, but for a couple of hours, I owned a Jaguar XKE. That was the last time we played guts. The rules for future poker games became No Guts Poker Nights!

CHAPTER 25

Really Fun Afternoon

In the early 1990s, the Board of Public Schools passed a very large bond issue that was matched by the federal government to pay for the addition of full-sized gymnasiums on all of the St. Louis schools, elementary as well as middle and high schools. The architectural department of the school system put out design parameters to equate the buildings that Architect William B. Ittner created in the early 1900s. William B. Ittner was a nationally recognized architect for his beautiful school designs, and his use of brick in exquisite complex patterns and colors were magnificent examples of the capability of brick in creating elegant and very beautiful facades. The Board of Education architects were to find brick that would match what Ittner used in the early twentieth century. This goal was right up our alley.

We, as all the other brick suppliers in St. Louis, were given the challenge of matching the brick on those schools built sixty to seventy years previously. My father, the founder of Missouri Brick Co., said that when he moved to St. Louis in 1926, there were twenty-five brick manufacturers within the city. In 1990, there were none. So matching the colors of those bricks used on those schools was indeed a challenge. There were close to fifty gymnasiums to be built, with quite a large amount of brick to be furnished, and we loved that challenge.

The school architects in charge of the additions, in order to be fair to all of the suppliers in the area would have what the lead architect, Scott Ritter, termed a "brick-off," where the brick suppliers in the area would gather at the site of the existing school and dry stack their best offering to match the brick in that particular building. These meeting times were generally around two o'clock in an afternoon on a day in mid-week. I was the brick matching specialist for my father's company, and fortunately of the first fifteen schools, we received the orders for thirteen of them. It was a difficult task, but we spent a great deal of time and effort in matching those old brick blends and colors.

Our main competitor was a company named Richard's Brick Co., and their sales person, Don Edris, put in a great effort to match the schools as well. We represented a brick manufacturer named Belden Brick Co. with their plants in Sugarcreek, Ohio, and their products more closely matched the old colors and textures that William B. Ittner used, so we were more successful in supplying the matching brick used on the schools. Don Edris really made a strong effort, but mostly failed. Don and I had never met in person; however, we were aware that we were strong opponents.

There was a brick-off at 2:00 p.m. on a school on South Broadway, very close to the Anheuser Busch world headquarters, which we also furnished using Belden Brick. I had arrived at noon and built what I felt was an almost perfect match. I was satisfied with the panel and left to grab a quick lunch before the meeting. I returned to the school at 1:30 to find another brick supplier with the trunk of his car loaded with brick, and he was constructing his mock-up to match the building. He had boxes of brick that said Richard's Brick Co., so I figured that the panel builder had to be Don Edris, my main opponent. Unlike most of the other brick peddlers in town, I always wore a suit or a sport coat with a white shirt and tie. I got out of my car and watched Don Edris constructing his panel for the 2:00 meeting.

After he finished his layup he, not knowing who I was, but I guess that I was looking sort of official in my suit and tie, he came up to me and said, "Which panel do you like?"

I replied, "They both look good, but I think the panel on the left is a better match, (mine) the panel on the right (his) needs a little more red." He went to his car trunk, tore down his panel, and rebuilt it with redder brick in his trunk while

I continued expressionlessly watching him in the ninety-plus degree weather putting the finishing touches on his "redder" panel. Satisfied with his new submittal he came back to me and very proudly said to me, "Well, what do you think now?"

I said "It is better, but I still prefer the panel on the left. The panel on the right needs more of those browner toned flashes."

Don, now sweating heavily, went back to his car again, tore down and reconstructed his panel adding more of those brown flashes. He finished it and said, "How about now?"

I said, "It is much improved, but I think the panel on the left nails it."

He looked at me with his sweaty and sagging shoulders and said, "I am Don Edris with Richard's Brick."

I replied, "Finally nice to meet you, sir, I'm Don Marquess."

His face went totally blank and his shoulders sagged even further and muttered a four letter expletive.

The school architects arrived and looked at both panels, and unanimously selected the panel on the left. Don Edris, got in his car and dejectedly drove away, probably to Anheuser Busch just down the street.

Just as a postscript to this delightedly devilish story, through our efforts, we furnished forty-three of the fifty-plus school additions.

Chapter 26

Twenty-Six? Why?

Good question, eh? Well, here is the reason: The number 26 is a significant number for me. I was born on the twenty-sixth, my mother was born on the twenty-sixth, my son was born on the twenty-sixth, and my grandmother was born on the twenty-sixth; therefore, it seems to me that the number 26 has a certain degree of importance in my life. Anything with twenty-six on it touches off a bell for me. I know that is silly, and I know it is truly meaningless; however, when I see the number 26 on anything my eyes light up and my ears perk up considerably.

Missouri Brick Co. was in the ceramic tile business as well as brick, and there was a ceramic tile distributor's convention in Reno, Nevada, at the MGM Grand in the early nineties. I was on the board of directors of that organization and was happy to attend the convention. It was a great event to see friends, establish some distributor guidelines, and perhaps snag a new line or two.

Three good friends of mine, Tom Brann from Chicago, Bill Haslett from Atlanta, and Suzy Stillson from Columbus, Ohio, were in attendance, and we met for lunch. It was a great lunch, and it was a pleasure to be with good friends again. At this lunch, we formed a limited partnership and the four of us contributed $30 each to invest in a slot machine that we would choose on the casino floor. The machine our LLC partnership chose was a typical bandit with the proper amount of bells and fire and smoke. It had an option of one or two coins. We had a board meeting to decide if it was a good time to pop for two coins or just stay with our twenty-five cents per spin investment. We were guessing correctly and doubled our corporate slot investment. Our initial buy in was $30 each ($120), and we now had over $250 for our newly formed corporation. One of our investors, Tom Brann, thought that we were pushing our luck, and we should unload our stash into one of those popcorn-like buckets and seek another machine for a while. This was such a fun adventure, and we initiated a search committee to find a new source of funding.

We all voted on several machines and finally agreed unanimously on a new bandit. Same thing as before, voting on one or two quarters, however not with the same profitable results. We lost a considerable amount of our profit, and with a motion before the board, we elected to return to the original machine, which we named Mom. We returned to Mom, and she continued bestowing us with great rewards. We loaded up and left Mom several more times, but always returned to Mom, and she was indeed very kind to the shareholders. Our $30 investment gave us over three hours of giggles and laughs, although we eventually went bankrupt (chapter 7), but what a fun-filled afternoon.

We agreed to gather back at Mom's for dinner at 5:00 p.m. So I went strolling and found an empty roulette table. The dealer was a very friendly guy and seemed to be happy to have someone play his game of chance. I guess everyone that gambles has some sort of system for whatever bet they make, and I do as well. I rarely play roulette, but when I do, my system is as follows: I start off with $1 on number 26 and place $1 on each corner. The odds on one number are 35:1. The odds on each corner surrounding number 26 are 8:1. So if any number from 22–30 hits on the spin of the wheel, I win something. After each spin of the wheel, I add $1 to each corner along with my number 26. On the first spin, I hit a corner $3.00 profit. The second spin now has $2.00 on each of the corners, plus the number 26 in the center. The second spin got another corner—that yielded a profit of $11. The third spin (a total now wagered of $15) got two corners, which pays 17:1, so I got $105–$15 netting a profit of $90. The fourth spin missed me completely, so $20 lost. I still have a profit of $84. The next spin hit number 26 with $5 on each corner along with $5 on number 26. Whoopee! That yielded $175 for the number ($5 x 35) plus 8 x $5 = $40 for each of the corners a total of $335. When a win occurs, the dealer pays you directly and leaves the original bet on the table. So as I am stacking my chips number 26 hits again. Good grief, another $335 with my cherished number 26 hitting twice in a row. I couldn't believe it, and you probably won't believe the rest of this story either, but it is very true.

I felt that I had pushed my luck just about as far as it could go, so I went to the cashier and cashed in $785. I got seven beautiful $100 bills and kept the $85 in chips. It was almost 5:00 p.m., time for me to meet the members of our LLC slot partnership, so I returned to our meeting place at the good mother slot machine, and met the three limited liability board members. I was so excited with my winnings that I led them to the roulette table of my great fortune, and as I walked up with my friends, the dealer said, "Well, here comes Mr. 26."

I told the complete story to my friends and took my $85 in chips, placed it on number 26, the dealer spun the wheel, and number 26 hit again—$2,975 win. I took that, plus the $85 wager, and cashed in $3060. This delightful bounty was added to those beautiful seven $100 bills, bringing my total catch for the day being $3,760. Deducting my $30 investment in the limited slot machine partnership, I still had a profit of $3,730. I bought dinner at the Asian restaurant in the hotel for the entire board (four people, including me) in our LLC slot corporation. My beloved number 26 hit three times in a row!

I didn't play roulette again for at least five years.

CHAPTER 27

English Is Hard

In my years as architectural representative for my father's brick company, I met many brilliant architects and artists. One of them was both, an architectural designer as well as a very talented artist. His name was Ralph Broughton. He designed many banks and commercial structures as well as providing art for the buildings. Ralph became a very good friend and presented me with one of the paintings I loved titled *Elaine*, you had to look closely, but after a few moments, you realize that *Elaine* is naked with a couple of her attributes clearly drawn. We had it hanging in the room where den mother, Susan, my wife, had several of her Cub Scout den meetings in front of that beautiful painting. When the cubbies discovered *Elaine's* beautiful body parts, the meetings were then moved to a different room. *Elaine* was better left alone.

Ralph also traveled to Mexico on occasion and discovered the bronze statues of a sculptor named Hernando Guernica, bought five, and offered me my choice. Since Susan loved horses so much, I chose the horse. It is a beautiful bronze, which is still in our living room. It was a gift from Ralph, which is still enjoyed in our house. Ralph was indeed a very good and generous friend.

Ralph for years pronounced his last name, Broughton, as in *though*. Then for some unknown reason, started pronouncing it *broughton* as in *bought*. He said that pronunciation was closer to the original English pronunciation. OK, I understood. But then I got to thinking, *Why stop there? There are other ways of pronouncing that grouping of letters (diphthongs?).*

It brought a mindboggling litany of possibilities:

He could elect to be named Bruffton, as in *tough*.

He could say he was Ralph Brooton, as in *through*.

He could become Ralph Browton, as in *thou*.

He could become Ralph Broffton, as in *cough*.

He could also become Ralph Bruppton, as in *hiccough* (hiccup).

I give up!

An artist (architectural renderer) friend of mine, Don Webb, whenever the three of us were going to lunch, which was often, would refer to Ralph as Mr. Brooton, Broughton, Broffton, Browton, or Bruppton. Even Ralph thought that was funny.

The Brits have always been the worst. How in the hell do you pronounce Gloucester, Maine, as *gloster*? Totally disregarding syllables as they choose. How about Worcester sauce? This way of thinking is far too exhausting to continue.

I would despise trying to learn English and think that Chinese would be the only way to go!

(All last night, I dreamed I was a tail pipe. I woke up exhausted)

Sorry about that one.

CHAPTER 28

Incredible Trust

My father started his brick business in 1960, and he rented space from a concrete block manufacturer located on Page Avenue in St. Louis County. The block storage yard was huge and had a rail siding. All the bricks at that came in by rail and had to be palletized by hand, which was a very hard work as a tong full of ten bricks weighed 40 lbs. or so and stacking five hundred bricks on a pallet was heavy labor. Thirty thousand or so bricks came in a boxcar, and unloading it would take my friends and I a couple of days to unload one. During the summer vacation, my friends and I spent many labor-intensive days between semesters, palletizing bricks. My arms and shoulders became somewhat massive.

One very hot July day, a man named Millard Hauck came into the office and told my dad he wanted to purchase a large amount of brick and wanted go through our yard to see what we had available. Millard had his ten-year-old or so son with him, and my dad and I went to the brickyard to show him the availability of what we had in stock. As we all went to view the brick we had on the yard, he would ask the quantity of each stack and would say, "OK, this will be fine, I'll take these," or "this is not enough, but I can use them for trim," and as we walked from pile to pile of brick, he was making his selections and building up quite a tab. We were really enjoying this brick excursion. Millard said he had a contract to build quite a few post offices in rural areas in Missouri, and my dad's new company was his first stop to buy brick.

As he was selecting another batch of brick, his son, who was picking up brick and looking at them and screamed in pain. As he was setting a brick back in the pile, he set it down too hard, and a brick chip flew and imbedded itself in the boy's right eye. His father told the boy to be calm as he inspected his eye. Sure enough in the white of his right eye was a very sharp chip of red brick. As his son was really hurting and in great pain, we went back up to the office, and the boy sat in the chair while really suffering.

His father said, "David, open your eye very wide and look to the ceiling." His son obeyed his father and did exactly what his father told him to do. His father reached into his pocket and pulled out a knife that my father termed a "frog sticker." It was a knife that had a 6" blade with a sharply pointed tip.

He said, "David, hold very still and don't move your eye at all." The father then put his hand on the cheek under his son's eye pulled it down while his son remained very still. Millard Hauck, using a very steady hand and with that sharply pointed knife, plucked the brick chip from his son's eye.

What incredible trust the son had in his father, and my dad and I were both amazed at the bond that existed between father and son. To this day, I tear up thinking about the total respect and trust that David had for his father, and the skill that his father had, and that he knew that his son would do exactly as instructed.

Afterward, Millard Hauck asked my dad for the total cost of the brick he selected. My dad did the calculation and the total was $15,850.

The man said, "Will you take $15,000 in cash?"

My dad said, "Sure!"

Millard went to his car and brought in a rather bulky brown Manila envelope and presented fifteen paper clipped sets containing ten $100 bills in each. He said he did his shopping for projects with $100,000 or so in cash because he always got the best deals paying in cash. How true!

My dad and I drove very carefully to the bank while feeling that every car we passed knew we had all that cash. When we got to the bank, we very nervously walked in and suspected that everyone knew we had it. We sat very close to the guard on duty. Once it was deposited, we drove back to the office fully relaxed.

Missouri Brick Co. has been in business for sixty-two years and has furnished brick to the most prestigious projects in the St. Louis area, Busch Stadium, huge hospital complexes, and countless schools and condominium projects. However, in all of those sixty-two years, no one paid as much as $15,000 in cold hard cash! Those two unforgettable moments happened on the same day way back in 1960.

CHAPTER 29
Mount St. Helens

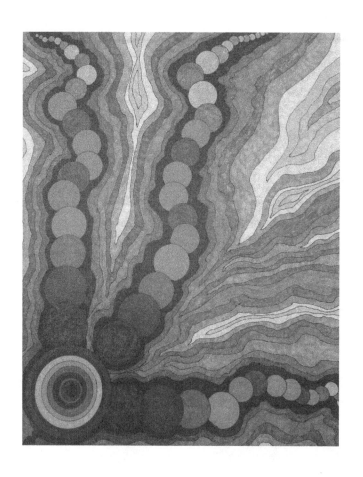

In most Cub Scout organizations, there are many events that are fund-raising projects for the pack. The Cub Scout pack at Tillman Elementary and Henry Hough middle school had mini car races called the Pinewood Derby and various other competitions. My son Donny won the Pinewood Derby in a triumph with a cigar made from the block of wood complete with the cigar label, and he beat all competitors. They also had cake-baking competitions where the rules were No Mother Participation. Donny won two of those with a turkey cake that looked exactly like a roasted turkey complete with a clear baker's glaze that made it look just like it just came out of the oven. A follow-up to that was a turkey dinner cake with all the trimmings. These cakes were auctioned with parents and guests bidding with fine rewards for the Cub Scout pack.

On the Fourth of July, there was another cake bake competition, and Danny, the younger son, wanted to make a big firecracker. Great idea! However, it was going to be a really big firecracker. We baked six layers of cakes to build this firecracker. As we were stacking the layers, when we got to the fourth layer, the cake started to sag, so I got some masking tape to hold it together. The fifth layer caused it to tilt further, so I went to my workshop and cut some wooden dowel rods to further support the layers. The sixth layer was another disaster. As we placed the top layer, it was revealed that I had cut the dowel rods about a half inch too long. So I went back down to my workshop to cut off about an inch from all four rods.

In the meantime, the cake had tilted much more, so more masking tape. The reinsertion of the dowel rods straightened the cake, and it looked ready for the shiny deep red icing. We iced the firecracker and stuck the six-inch piece of clothesline for the wick, and the cake was indeed a beautiful sight to behold. It was ready for the auction, and the den mother gave it a lot of hype and stated that it indeed would be a great value since it was six layers tall. One lucky bidder paid $16.50 for that firecracker. I felt that I needed to explain a few of the hidden supports to the buyer, so I revealed the masking tape and dowel rods that he was also getting as a bonus. As I was explaining these issues to him, I was laughing all the way; however, the purchaser had zero sense of humor, and the more I revealed, the more I laughed, but the more sour his expression became. This individual apparently didn't appreciate the hoodwinking we perpetrated, so I offered to reimburse him for his bad investment. That bum took it. We took the firecracker home and after disassembling all of the extras, the cake tasted rather good.

The next cake-baking contest was the summer of 1980, the year of the March twenty-seventh eruption of Mt. St. Helens. Danny decided that we should bake a volcano. Terrific idea for winning another prestigious award in his glorious history of competing in Cub Scout events. I had the brilliant idea of placing a little votive candle cup at the top of the volcano with several of those little black snakes inserted so that when the snakes were ignited, a spew erupted with black snake foam ashes that greatly resembled lava. It was certainly going to be another victory to be added to his stellar list of his Cub Scout awards. The evening of the competition with Mt. St. Helens on display and ready to be ignited when the judges came to view, Danny was telling several of his friends about the impending eruption and how his cake would again win the top prize. He lit the black snakes and the very acrid smoke started spewing as the snakes were erupting. The gymnasium became filled with this terrible smoke, and it had to be evacuated and all of the windows were opened in the hope of clearing the smoke from the hall. It was indeed a brilliant idea that wasn't thought completely through.

The volcano was just as hoped, but the outcome was not as desired.

CHAPTER 30

1982 McDonnell Douglas Aero Classic

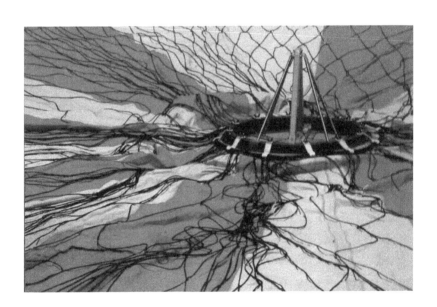

My photographs graced the pages of the program for the Great Forest Park Balloon Race for several years, and I was enjoying the experience to photograph that event. My photos were used exclusively in the official balloon race program. In actuality, whenever there was an unsold space in the program, one of my photos was inserted and I received photo credit. One year all spaces were sold, so none of my photos were used; nevertheless, I received credit for all photos in the program, when none were there.

Each year, there were seventy-five to eighty hot-air balloons in that event, and it was touted as the largest viewed balloon launching in the country. However, the balloons did fly over the St. Louis Metropolitan Area, consisting of almost 3 million people. I also had the opportunity to photograph the Big Balloon Event with over seven hundred balloons in Albuquerque, New Mexico. Albuquerque has what is referred to as the Albuquerque Box, which means that due to wind currents, a balloon may be launched to ascend to an altitude and be carried by the wind for a couple of miles or so, then descend to a lower altitude, catch a different wind current, and be transported back to the starting point.

It should be pointed out that balloons rule the skies. Since the only control that balloons have is altitudinal, they can only go up or down depending on the heat in the envelope (the big balloon itself), and they are at the mercy of wind currents. All aircraft must give precedence to balloons. A hot-air balloon is heated by propane tanks directly over the transport basket, the gondola, and the hot air in the envelope causes the balloon to rise. This usually takes a crew of three to four people laying the balloon out and preparing it to receive the hot air created by the heat from the propane burner. They usually volunteer in exchange for the hope of being offered a ride in the future. A balloon ride is indeed a wonderful pleasure, and I have been fortunate to ride in one five times. In fact, if I were offered a ride from one landing on my front lawn today, I would jump in and take an hour or so ride. It is an experience not to be missed. Gas balloons, however, are a completely different situation.

The inflation of a gas balloon is a totally different inflation process. A gas balloon is the type that can fly for hours, up to days, not hours. They fly at altitudes up to 18,000 ft. (three and a half miles), while a hot-air balloon only flies at three thousand feet max. The cost today for a hot-air balloon is thirty to forty thousand dollars. The cost for a gas balloon is $250,000 plus. Also the time to fill a gas balloon with helium or hydrogen is $3,200 - $5,000. A gas balloon takes a major financial commitment and usually has a corporate sponsor.

In 1982, there was a huge gas balloon event in St. Louis at Laclede's Landing close to the Mississippi River. There were eight giant gas balloons participating in the event being sponsored by McDonnell Douglas (now Boeing), with the projected target being the Washington Monument in our nation's capital for landing. The gas being supplied for the event was helium that cost over $25,000, about $3,000 per balloon, and was being paid for by McDonnell. Sandy McDonnell himself was on hand for the event. So was I, as the photographer.

The balloon guru in St. Louis was a fine lady named Nicki Caplan, who also instituted the Great Forest Park Balloon Race, and she had a gas balloon entered in the event. At this time, Nikki was giving hot-air balloon instructions to her student Flip Wilson who was also in town to view the launching. We had a pre-event screening of my hot air balloon photos, with accompanying music, at the St. Louis Planetarium. Flip Wilson, wearing his stark white Nehru jacket, kept us all entertained with his stories as the reverend of the "Church of What's Happening Now," and his Emmy-winning character, Geraldine, famous for, as she explained to her husband, the church pastor, "The devil made me buy this dress . . . I didn't want to do it, but the devil *made* me buy this dress."

For you youngsters reading this book, Flip was at the top of his game with several Emmy's and Grammy's under his belt due to his unique approach to comedy. The balloonists and crews in the theater seemed to enjoy Flip's humor even more than my photos. This was a very important event that captured national attention in the ballooning world.

Filling a hot-air balloon takes around an hour with three to four assistants. Filling a gas balloon can take six hours plus and ten or so volunteers. Most of the volunteers usually have no experience with hot-air balloons, much less with gas balloons, and are quickly schooled with on the job training. With a gas balloon, there is a netting covering the envelope with ballast bags about the size of a quart size bottle of milk. These bags are filled with sand for holding the balloon on the earth during the filling of gas before going aloft. As the gas is sent to the balloon through the umbilical, the balloon envelope begins to inflate and rise slowly. The volunteers are surrounding the balloon, and as it begins rising, they are instructed to lower the sandbag ballast gently from netting square down to the next netting square while always keeping the bags hooked for holding the balloon securely on the ground.

A frightening and very costly occurrence happened as these volunteers started having fun dropping the sandbags from hooking spot to hooking spot as the envelope was rising. These kids seemed to enjoy dropping the bags instead of gently moving them down from netting square to netting square. When all of a sudden, I heard a snap, snap, snap, and a chain reaction occurred as all the bags dropped to the ground and Nikki Caplan's balloon took off with no pilot and no passenger. It was a complete disaster!

Sandy McDonnell quickly ran to his car and called his company to scramble and launch two phantom jets to chase and surround the balloon to inform other aircraft of the hazard in the sky. All other airborne craft had to be aware of that balloon with no pilot, rising in the sky. (I thought at the time, what absolute power he had to just make a phone call and launch two phantom jets.)

That balloon traveled to Iowa where it crash-landed, destroying the balloon and instruments totaling close to $100,000.

Nevertheless, master balloon pilot Nikki Caplan continued to rack up more and more awards and was given the Top Woman Balloonist in the World title and was enshrined in the National Balloonist Hall of Fame in Indianola, Iowa, on July 27, 2014. Nikki Caplin was like the unsinkable Molly Brown. She wouldn't let a little loss of a $100,000 balloon slow her up even a little bit!

Chapter 31

OFB 2003

If you are a baseball fan, spring training is an experience not to be missed. The stadiums are much smaller than the major league stadiums, (six to seven thousand compared to thirty-five to fifty thousand capacity), so almost every seat is closer to the action. There are very few two-tiered stadiums for spring training games, and the entire atmosphere is more laid-back than major league stadiums. Every game is more relaxed than the intensity of a major league game. Granted, the games outcomes are meaningless since none of the games count in the regular season; however, many hopeful players are given an opportunity to showcase their talents in the hope of getting noticed and to be included on the major league rosters. A minor league player may make $15,000 to $35,000 a year, while the minimum salary for a major league player is $720,000. A major, major difference for a player to jump from the minors to the majors, so the pressure for a player is gigantic. Marty Hendin with the Cardinals told that the major league traveling meal money is more than a minor league makes in a month. While the experience is laid back for the fans, it is very intense for the young aspirants.

Just as an example, every high school in the country has a baseball team. That is an unbelievable amount of players hoping to be one of the eight hundred fortunate baseball players in the MLB. Showing the difficulty of hitting major league pitching, a player that fails seven out of ten times to hit a baseball, makes $20,000,000 per year. Failing seven out of ten times means that player hits three hundred, which is the definition of an elite player. That shows that hitting a baseball is the single most difficult thing to do in all major sports. My good friend, photographer Lewis Portnoy, who was chosen to be on the USA Olympic team of photographers for four Olympics, said that without question, hitting a baseball is a more difficult action than any other sport accomplishment. If a player has that talent to put the round bat on the round ball, heading to him at ninety miles per hour or more. The pot of gold awaits. Spring training is the time to show talents to those who make a thumbs up or thumbs down decision regarding those with talents hoping to make the big league team. Spring training is indeed a laid-back and easy experience for the fans, but a much more intense situation for aspiring players.

Being a baseball art photographer for eleven spring trainings, I was invited to attend the games by the vice president of the Cardinals, Marty Hendin. Later years, that invitation was given to me by John Rooney, Cardinals broadcaster. My photos were being sold in the team store at Roger Dean Stadium in Jupiter, Florida. Seven of my prints were sold with the request that I sign them. Lou Brock and Bob Gibson were having a signing in a private room after a spring training game in 2003. Marty Hendin set it up that I would be signing my prints next to Brock and Gibson.

Lou Brock was signing his items, balls, cards, jerseys, etc. He was signing his name and below his name signing "HOF

1985," Bob Gibson was signing his name with "HOF 1981." HOF was the year of induction to baseball's Hall of Fame in Cooperstown, New York, a very exclusive honor, and since its inception only 269 players as of 2023 have been inducted.

I was sitting next to Lou Brock, who was including his HOF 1985 induction on each item he signed. I started signing mine Don P. Marquess, OFB 2003. Lou, in between his signings noticed that I was signing my prints with the OFB 2003 under my name and kept looking, trying to figure what the OFB stood for, and eventually asked, "Don, what does the OFB mean?"

I said "Old, Fat, and Broke 2003."

Chapter 32

The Sparkling Hawaiian Rainbow

I was fortunate to travel to Germany twice in one year, as well as a trip or two to Phoenix in the same twelve-month period. TWA airlines, at that time, was headquartered in St. Louis, and announced a program that for traveling four international segments and four domestic segments within a calendar year would receive two first-class round trips to anywhere TWA flew. I was only two segments short. I found the cheapest round trip from St. Louis to anywhere, which was to Columbus, Ohio, for $122.00, so I booked it. There was a delay of two and a half hours before the return trip to St. Louis, so I jumped on board.

Two free first class round trips to anywhere TWA flew was an offer not to be missed. All I had to do was convince my beautiful wife, Susan, to forget her fear of flying and accompany me on a trip anywhere she desired for free! A major convincing job was needed.

"Not now, dear, the boys are in school now, and I can't leave them now," "No, this is not a good time, let's plan on it later," "Not now, my sister wants to visit us this year, and I don't know when she can make it," "Who will feed the cat?"

Excuse after excuse. No matter what, it was apparent that she was not getting on a plane for any reason! In 1999, TWA said that all free flights must be taken before the end of 2001 or they would be lost forever. I checked with TWA who said that my two free tickets could be taken on two separate flights. I realized that my dream of Susan and I going together was a hopeless goal, so I knew that one of those trips would be to Hawaii. I had been to forty-eight states with the two missing states being the hardest to get to, and going to Hawaii would leave only Alaska in my quest for traveling to all fifty states. So Hawaii, here I come. Ticket number 2 would be decided later. Trip number 2 was later chosen to be in October 2001 to Cairo, Egypt; however, after the 9/11/01 disaster, all trips to the Middle East were cancelled.

My first class ticket to Hawaii included a stop in Los Angeles with about a two-hour-or-so wait before the flight to the big island of Hawaii. The gate area in the Los Angeles airport was a very large circular room with six or so other gates. My flight showed it would be on-time leaving at 2:35 p.m. My flight there landed at 12:30, so I had time for lunch and a little stroll. I kept passing by that gate showing 2:35 p.m. departure. but there were no attendants nor passengers lining up. So I continued to walk around the area and entered a small bookstore (I am a bookworm) and surveyed the latest publications. No matter how hard I tried, or how many books I read, more books were published than I could read every year, so I made notes of what I would put in my reading queue. Then returning to the gate again at 2:20 and seeing no activity at the gate, I was getting worried that maybe the flight was cancelled. I walked around another few minutes then went directly to the gate, and there was a sign at the gate that the entry had been moved to down the hallway, not at the gate desk. I almost ran down the hallway just in time to see my plane take off. My luggage and everything was on the way to Hawaii, and my first-class seat was empty. I explained my error to the personnel at the makeshift gate, and thankfully they were sympathetic. Another flight was leaving the next day at the same time, and they made a reservation for me to have the same seat. They even made a TWA-paid reservation at a nearby Holiday Inn for the night.

I was at the airport the next day in plenty of time, and the same gate was there with attendants, so this time I actually got on the plane and sat in my first-class seat while hoping that my luggage of two suitcases would be located when I arrived. As I exited the plane at Kona airport on the big island of Hawaii, I saw my luggage being wheeled to the lost luggage area. I flagged down the attendant and captured my luggage. This airport was small and very open with no big closed-in building, and with the beautiful lei, now around my neck, I was well aware that I had indeed reached paradise. The temperature was a very comfortable eighty-five degrees, and I was thrilled to finally arrive.

I had rented a condo right on the beach a mile or so from the airport, and I was hoping it wasn't occupied by someone else; but then again, I already paid for it for eight days, so I assumed they didn't care if I ever showed up. The condo was directly on the ocean, and I could only see the beach if I leaned over the balcony (Lanai). I had purchased an island-hopper ticket before I left the mainland (which was the only way you could get one at that time) from Aloha Airlines that cost under $300, if I remember correctly. I think it was actually $299. It was a first class ticket with unlimited travel between the islands. All I had to do was show up at the airport, show the pass, and get on the plane. I don't think that is still available, but what a great bargain. The big island, Hawaii, actually has just about everything Hawaii has to offer, a volcano, a coffee plantation, a rain forest, a pineapple plantation (I was surprised to see how short pineapple trees were), great hotels, and dining. I traveled around the island several times in the PT Cruiser that I had rented for the week. The weather was spectacular, and I did everything that I could squeeze in in one week's time. I rode in a submarine, went deep-sea fishing, rode in a helicopter around the big island, and dined very well at several Luau events. I had a wonderful dinner at the Orchid Resort and Spa. They set up a table for me right on the edge of the beach, I ordered dinner, and I saw a man in swimming shorts with a green leaf headband, run out to the edge of the rocks, and blow a long note on a conch shell signaling sunset. Immediately thereafter, I heard a guitar playing and turned to my right, and there was a gorgeous young lady in a grass skirt dancing in front of a Hawaiian guitarist. I looked around for someone to pinch me, as I felt that surely, I was dreaming. However, the highlight of this trip was yet to come . . .

My trip the next morning was to the Island of Kauai, which was another gorgeous island paradise. The Waimea Canyon on the island was breathtaking with lush trees and greenery and a spectacular waterfall. It was a photographer's dream, and I burned a generous amount of Fuji Velvia film.

As I was departing the canyon a rainstorm hit and somehow or another, it appeared from a clear blue sky. I guess I truly was dreaming. The rain stopped almost as quickly as it started, and in the distance ahead of me on the road was a beautiful rainbow. Rainbows always seem to get further away the closer you get, but not this time. The closer I got to the rainbow, the closer I got to the rainbow. The road was approaching a creek at the bottom of the hill, and the rainbow didn't disappear and remained straight ahead of me. As I got to the base of the hill crossing the creek the rainbow still remained, and as I drove through it, little dewdrops of multicolors were sparkling out the window on the passenger side of my car. It was incredible, and I was almost shaking. At the top of the hill, there was a pull off at the side of the road, and I stopped there to catch my breath. A white pickup truck pulled in next to me, and a man jumped out of the cab with eyes almost as large as billiard balls said to me, "Wow . . . Did you see that rainbow we both drove through?"

He said, "I moved here from the state of Oregon fifteen years ago, and I have never seen anything like that in my life." Needless to say, neither had I.

A year or so later, a lovely lady from Hawaii was in my gallery in St. Louis, and I told her my story of driving through that sparkling rainbow with the multicolored dew like drops. She looked astounded and said, "That is called the hoonimakkeewanie rainbow (or something like that), and it is an island legend. If you drive through it, you will have great luck for life." I have never found proof of that legend, but she may have been right. I am eighty-two years old and writing my second book, and have had an incredibly gifted life. However, I have yet to win the lottery. That will happen when I drive through the next rainbow. Hopefully before I am struck by a lightning bolt.

— CHAPTER 33 —

The Remarkable Marty

Marty Hendin was the most incredible catalyst I ever met in my life. Marty was always putting two people together to make things happen. "You need to speak with Melvin Schmidlap, who produces products that could utilize your gizmos." Marty always knew who did what and who could benefit from a mutual relationship. Marty introduced me to

Jack Buck, the Hall of Fame broadcaster, who, in his latter years, became a very fine and prolific poet. Marty told Jack that he should incorporate his poems on my photos, and we could produce posters that would enable fans to purchase prints that contained nice backgrounds for Jack's poems. We produced seven posters together that sold very well. Marty was a great catalyst indeed.

Marty Hendin was vice president of Community Relations for St. Louis Cardinals and the greatest ambassador for baseball ever, especially for Cardinals baseball. Marty and I had lunch once a week for over ten years. On the way to the restaurant, we talked about baseball. During lunch, we talked the about the Cardinals, and on the way back to his office, we talked about Cardinals baseball. Marty was always promoting the Cardinals and was on the board of at least ten charities, and constantly succeeding in raising funds for each of them.

Many times when a person is approached for a charitable donation, the individual, if indeed donating, afterward would think to himself, *Why in the hell did I just give my money away?* However, it's not like that with Marty. He always made you feel important and very fortunate to donate.

"Boy was I lucky Marty asked me." Marty had that incredible talent to make people feel very fortunate in giving their money away. Marty also had that unique talent that never offended anyone nor made them feel that they were just fleeced. Marty was also very impressive in stature being 6'5" tall. Maybe deep down inside, people had a comfort in acquiescence.

Due to Marty's very friendly nature, and being the VP of community relations, anytime a celebrity came to a Cardinals game, Marty Hendin's office was a necessary stop. In Marty's office, I met innumerable celebrities. Marty's office was a very enjoyable stop after every Cardinals game. I met Rob Reiner,

Kenny Rogers, Bob Uecker, and Tony Orlando, among many others.

It was always after a game, and it just didn't seem right if I didn't stop at Marty's office. Usually there was a celebrity of some sort, or a great looking blonde, or some beautiful lady involved in a charitable endeavor. One day in the fifth inning of a Cards/Cubs game, Marty called me on my cell phone and said that I had to come to his office immediately. Well, I knew that it would be someone very famous, or at least some incredible-looking babe, so I hotfooted to his office, anticipating a meeting with someone special. As I entered his office, there was just a nice-looking lady in her mid-thirties, wearing a blue tee shirt with the red and white big *C* of the Chicago Cubs logo. She was just a nice-appearing lady, but not a celebrity nor a bombshell. I wondered just why Marty said I had to meet her.

Marty said to her, "Please turn around so Don can see the back of your tee."

She turned around.,and on the back of the shirt, it said, "Chicago Cubs . . . Heck, any team can have a bad century."

Marty had a love-hate relationship with the Cubbies. He loved them to come to St. Louis for the Cubs/Cards games, but he hated them to win, which fortunately was a rarity.

Every year for over ten years, Susan and I went on the Cardinals Cruise. There were always very interesting Ports of Call and the cruises were very much fun. One such cruise took us to the island of St. Thomas, which was probably the most beautiful island in the Caribbean. We took a cab to the top of a storybook mountain overlooking a gorgeous, deep, and very verdant valley. There was a wall with a railing at the end of a terrace outside the gift shop. The drop must have been close to one thousand feet or so. As we were standing and taking in the beauty of this wondrous valley, a young lady wearing a Chicago Cubs shirt walked between us and leaned against the railing while taking photographs of this beautiful sight. Marty looked at me, looked at her, and stared over the railing at the very long and very deep valley. Marty looked at me again, stared at the valley, and kind of nodded his head at the lady, then at the valley, then at me again. Then the lady walked away. Marty looked at me and said, "Mr. Marquess, we both missed a great opportunity to thin out an alien fan base!"

I went to spring training with Marty every spring for many years, and he always gave a ticket to the visiting celebrity next to me behind home plate. I sat with John Goodman, John Pizzarelli, George McGovern, and Leonard Slatkin. One of the guests was Bruce Adler who was a major Cardinals fan as well as an incredibly talented singer and actor. Bruce and I became very good friends and had lunch together on his visits to St. Louis. He was a very close friend of Marty's. One spring training he was starring in a one-man show at a theater in Ft. Lauderdale when he told this hysterically funny joke:

A man was visiting a loved one at a cemetery when he heard a man sobbing. He looked around and saw a man kneeling at a gravestone and crying very loudly while banging his fist on the grave and screaming, "Why did you have to die, oh why did you have to die?"

The man walked up to him and tried to comfort him. He said, "Oh, sir, I am so sorry for you."

The kneeling man continued sobbing and saying, "Why did you have to die . . . oh why did you have to die?"

The man was totally pitiful and just couldn't stop wailing and banging his fist on the grave. The man asked him who it was that died. The sobbing man said again while banging his fist on the grave, "Why did you have to die, oh why did you have to die?"

He then looked at the man who was trying to comfort him and said to him, "It was my wife's first husband!"

CHAPTER 34

Tornado Encounters

In our first house in Kirkwood we had a garden room on the south side of our Cape Cod style one and a half story home. That garden room was my favorite room in the house. It was a converted sunroom that had beautiful white handmade ceramic tile on the floor. During a snowfall or a rainstorm, it was a wonderful experience looking out of the three walls of windows while being warm and snug inside. One such evening in August, while enjoying the movie *Elephant Walk* with Elizabeth Taylor and Dana Andrews, there was a vicious rainstorm occurring outside. It got even heavier and then suddenly stopped, and the air in the house became very heavy. I felt incredible pressure and several doors in the house blew open. Then I heard a train. It actually did sound like a train, then a big thump on the house that shook the walls and all the lights went out. Yikes! Susan was in the kitchen, and we ran to each other, considerably frightened. Donny, the four-year-old, came finding his way down the stairs as I was going up the stairs to check on our one-year-old Danny. Danny was standing up in his crib with eyes as large as teacups, not looking frightened, just wondering what the dickens happened.

I picked him up, held him tight, and said that we just had a terrific storm. I carried him downstairs to be with Susan and Donny as we all just relaxed, took a deep breath, and tried to survey the damage.

I looked out the back of the porch to our backyard, and one of the twin oaks was gone. There were two before the storm. I looked further in our yard and found that giant oak lying across our neighbor's fence on the north side of our property. That mighty oak was no challenge to that strong wind. The rain picked up again, and the Kirkwood tornado sirens began blasting. (A little late for sure.) Then our front doorbell rang. I answered it to find a fireman in his rain-soaked yellow coat asking if we were all right. I told him, "Yes, but pretty much shaken up, and we were slowly calming down."

Until a tornado touches the ground, it is just a funnel cloud. Only when it touches the earth does it become a tornado. The taller one of our twin oaks in back was high enough for that funnel cloud to grab it and twist it out of the ground, bounce it off our roof, hit our power lines, then land across our neighbor's fence. The next morning, as I further inspected the damage, the stump from the oak tree was twisted in the ground. I then understood more fully the term "twister."

I had heard that many people say that a tornado sounds like a train. It truly does, and a mighty big train at that!

The other encounter is very unusual as well. We were headed to Interlochen, Michigan, to visit our son Donny who was performing piano concertos at the National Music Camp. We were in Illinois on Highway 52, heading north to Michigan. There were many layers of gray and dusty blue-colored clouds in the sky, and two of those cloud layers had a connector of a white cylinder, like an umbilical cord, in the center of those two layers. This cloud formation was maybe five or six miles ahead of us, but Susan and I both felt that those clouds really looked mean. We kept driving while keeping our eyes on those two layers of clouds with that white umbilical between them. The distance between the clouds slowly separated as we were watching, and that white connector suddenly broke through the bottom cloud. I will always remember seeing the cotton candy-like swirl looking like white and gray spinning together. I immediately pulled to the side of the road, and the three of us jumped out of the car and laid together in a ditch as that twisting mass crossed the highway not more than five hundred feet ahead of us. Being a photographer, I had three cameras in the trunk, but not one in my hand to take a photo of the actual formation of that tornado that crossed the road directly in front of us. It kicked up a lot of dust and traveled East through Northern Illinois, tearing up land and vegetation.

I feel that we saw what meteorologists and storm chasers never get a chance to see—the actual formation of a tornado. Lucky us(?). We saw one form, although we never were transported to that wonderful Land of Oz.

CHAPTER 35

Wonderful Pranks

In my career of being an architectural representative for my father's company, Missouri Brick Co., I was fortunate to meet many remarkable individuals. One such individual was Joe Drachnik. Joe was a graduate of Washington University and possessed two engineering degrees, electrical and architectural. Joe was a delight to be with, and we had lunch together on many occasions. Joe was a spec writer and associate with HOK architects (Helmuth, Obata, and Kassabaum), one of the top architectural firms in the world. It was at one of our luncheons he told me this outrageous prank.

One of Joe's good friends worked in the accounting department at McDonnell Douglas, the producer of fighter jets in St. Louis. The Phantom F4 was one of the most versatile jet aircrafts in the world, and they were produced in the St. Louis plant, which employed over ten thousand people. It was so large. It was like another city. Joe's friend said that one of the accountants had purchased a Volkswagen Beetle and continually bragged about the incredible gas mileage he was getting on his new car. With American cars getting eleven to thirteen miles per gallon, his new Beetle was getting over twenty miles per gallon. With his constantly talking about it to his fellow workers, they devised this wonderful prank.

At lunch several of his coworkers would bring cans of gas and secretly add gas to the Beetle. Being an accountant and excellent with calculations, the Beetle owner would continue regaling his office buddies about the remarkable gas mileage he was getting from his auto.

"You won't believe this guys, I am getting over thirty miles per gallon."

"Yeah, yeah," his coworkers responded, "we are getting tired of hearing that."

The office guys had so much fun with the prank, they intensified the adding of fuel. The Beetle owner, against the pleading of his coworkers, just couldn't stop bragging about his gas mileage.

"It is just flat unbelievable guys, I am getting over fifty-five miles per gallon!".

"Oh come on. That is ridiculous, how can you be getting fifty-five miles per gallon?"

"Look, you guys, I know how to calculate mileage, and it is a fact!"

The office guys continued until over seventy miles per gallon was achieved. The owner lightened up on his wonderment and stopped his aggravating boasting.

The pranksters had so much fun doing that, they decided to do the opposite for a while and started siphoning gas from the Beetle. The owner stopped bragging about his gas mileage and didn't mention the incredible drop in miles per gallon. It must have dropped so low that he was probably getting under ten miles per gallon.

The owner took the car back to the dealer and said, "There is something drastically wrong with this vehicle, I was getting over seventy miles per gallon, and now I'm getting under ten."

The service manager just stared at him like he was a four year old.

When the owner told his coworkers about his dilemma, they revealed their delicious prank!

At the same lunch, while on the subject of remarkable happenings, Joe told me of this incredible money-grabbing situation. A man took an ad in several major publications, including the *Wall Street Journal*, stating the start of his new company. His company was an investment company not listed on any stock exchange whatsoever, and he was offering shares in his company for $25 per share. In the ad, he stated that "The US government guarantees that after ten years, you won't lose your investment." Joe Drachnik then said the man took the $25 per share in his company, and purchased a savings bond for $18.75 with maturity in ten years and sent it to the "investors" in his company, thereby pocketing the $6.25 for himself. According to Joe, this entrepreneur made over $430,000 in the shares he sold. He was stopped only because he couldn't use the federal government in advertising to further a private enterprise.

True or not, that was an incredible story.

Joe, also at that very lunch, posed this question: "What does an insomniac, dyslexic agnostic do?"

"He stays awake all night wondering if there really is a dog."

CHAPTER 36

Very Hot Stuff

have always enjoyed hot spicy food, especially Mexican and Asian foods. I have two very good friends, Don Hussman and Dwight Dickinson, who are prominent and very successful architects in the St. Louis Metropolitan area, and they enjoy the spicier Mexican flair as well. We enjoy many lunches together and spend most of the time laughing while lunching. There was a new restaurant in Kirkwood (one of the 110 independent communities surrounding St. Louis) named Caliente', and we were up for trying it out.

During lunch, while awaiting our lunch specials of enchiladas, frijoles, and tacos, I started relating my love for hot spicy foods, and of one particular dining experience that I had months previously. There was a restaurant owned by ex-footballers with the St. Louis Football Cardinals, Dan Dierdorff and Jim Hart, named Jim and Dan's Rio Grande. It was one of the latest restaurants created by them and managed by my good friend Kenny Bland. Kenny was the food expert, and Jim and Dan were the money experts. A beautiful combination indeed.

Since it was very close to a movie theater that Susan and I frequented, we decided to try it out before the movie. The menu was Tex-Mex flair and all the dishes sounded scrumptious. I am a chili lover, and they had four choices from which to choose: American Chili, Tex-Mex Chili, Grandma's White Bean Chili, and Buzzard's Breath Chili. Buzzard's Breath Chili rang the proper bell for me, so I ordered a bowl. It was delivered to the table, I took a spoonful, it tasted just fine, so I took another spoonful, then the fire attacked. I am telling Don and Dwight about the horror and killer power of Buzzard's Breath as our lunch plates arrived. The plates were very attractively presented, and there was little red pepper on the side that was placed on the outside edge of the plate. I continued relating the Buzzard's Breath experience to them in telling them of my heroism in swallowing that second spoonful, and that it was the hottest thing I had ever tasted in my life.

I told them that the next morning, I called my friend Kenny Bland and left a message to call me in room number 402 of the burn unit at Barnes Hospital and left my cell phone number. Kenny called me very concerned shortly thereafter and said, "My god, Don, what happened?"

I said, "I had a bowl of your Buzzard's Breath Chili. There may be a lawsuit!"

Then as I am telling this story, I bit in half that little red pepper on the side of the plate. My entire life started flashing before me, but I was way too macho to readily admit that death was rapidly approaching. So I continued momentarily before it became apparent that if I didn't have a fire extinguisher immediately, my life was over. I could barely breathe and was gasping for air as we all summoned the waiter. He responded, looked at my wretched condition, and noticed the half-eaten pepper on my plate.

He said, "You didn't eat that, did you? It was a fresh Habenero pepper. We just got them in this morning for plate decoration."

"Wait a minute," I said while gasping for air, "this is lunchtime. I ordered food. It was on my plate. What am I supposed to do with it . . . say hi?"

Dwight and Don realized that if I died at that time, the lunch check was theirs, so they made every effort to save me and ordered a large glass of milk and a scoop of ice cream to assist in my survival. Thanks to them, I survived and I am able to relate this story.

Kenny Bland, in defense of the Buzzard's Breath of Death said that it was made with a combination of Jalapeños and Habeneros, but I was the only one who ordered it that day. It was made at 11:00 a.m., and this was 6:00 p.m.. It sat cooking down all day and all that survived were the peppers and a scant amount of meat and beans. Luckily I survived that as well.

CHAPTER 37

I Don't Gamble. I Play Poker

From the time I was a child, I enjoyed playing card games. My mom, dad, and brother played a game called pit, which as I remember was a game with cards that you traded commodities like flax (I never knew what that was . . . and still don't), wheat, oats, rice, etc. It was a somewhat a wild game with hands grabbing, cards flying until someone would yell "cornered on corn!" We also played a card game named authors, which I remember to this day regarding who wrote what. It was a very fun learning experience.

When the entire nation went goofy over a card game called Canasta, which was played with a double deck, and our whole family played it nightly for a while. My dad loved a game of cards called pinochle, which we played with his friends. I was always invited to play because of my card sense as my dad called it. We also played hearts, which was a game where you could wipe out all the opponents if you collected all thirteen hearts along with the kiss of death queen of spades. Every heart penalized you one point, and the queen of spades penalized you thirteen points. Unless you got all hearts and that dreaded queen, then all other players got charged twenty-six points against them. When you amassed one hundred points, you lost the game. I have a pretty good memory for cards, and a lot of my friends call it card sense. My brother, when I was just six or seven, would play a game with me called concentration, where all fifty-two cards were laid randomly on the table face down and you would expose one and try to match it with another—six with a six, eight with an eight, one at a time. Every time one card was exposed, you had to remember where the match was in the unexposed face down cards. So if another matching card was picked from the pile, you knew where its partner was. Whoever ended up with the most pairs, won the game. I consistently beat my ten years older brother.

In my twenties, there was a weekly (or maybe multiple times weekly) poker game with friends that floated from house to house. We played for high stakes of a $.25 limit—that is 25 cents being the most you could wager any time. Also a massive wager like that was a rarity. If you lost $25, it was a major catastrophe, except for one night at L. D. Brodsky's house.

We were playing seven card stud, and on the first five cards, I had a club flush. Terrific, eh? Not so fast. Barry on the first five cards had kings full. I was clearly toast. The other three players kept calling whatever we bet. I knew for certain I had won the pot. Not true. At that moment, I was a very sad second.

In seven card stud, the last card is face down, and it was dealt. I didn't look at mine, and neither did Barry look at his. We both knew we were golden with our hands. He bet everything he had, which was a little over $55 bucks (which was allowed on the last card). I knew I had won with my club flush, and I had around $60 dollars, so I called. He turned his cards over and revealed his kings full house. I knew I had lost, sadly. I turned my cards over, and the last card down was the seven of clubs, giving me a straight flush, a big surprise to us both. Barry, mustering as much control as he possibly could, stood up, smiled, and said, "I am never playing poker again!" Which was very true until the next week when we played again!

Now with the immense popularity of Texas hold 'em, I have developed a friendship with a very congenial group of friends, and we play every Sunday morning after breakfast at the Hollywood Casino in Maryland Heights, Missouri. Poker is an enormous challenge and greatly unpredictable. Just this afternoon, I had a diamond king high straight flush, which is extraordinary, and in the pot was only $10; however, I received an additional $325 from the house. The games are different, and every hand is unique. Poker is *not* a game playing against the house. You are playing against the other players. There are two exceptional players, Matt and Mike, who seem to win with remarkable consistency, and six or so others—Darryl, Goldie, Brian, Gregg, and Inky. There are very few major disasters, and generally a good time is had by all.

The worst hand I ever had was pocket queens and the flop was QQK. I had four queens, I bet $5, and everyone dropped. I didn't sleep for a couple nights as I should have checked, and let the hand develop.

Poker is a great game and somewhat addictive. I still remember cards as I did playing concentration with my brother.

CHAPTER 38

Fernando Tatis and the Incredible Feat

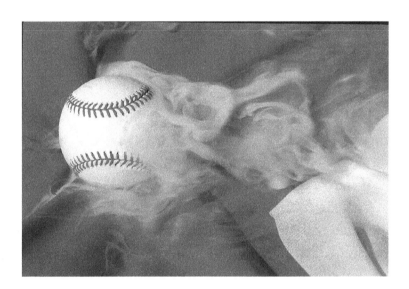

The date was April 23,1999, and the Cardinals were playing a night game that Friday in Los Angeles. The Cardinals were batting in the top of the third inning with the score 2-0 Dodgers. The Cardinals loaded the bases with two singles and a hit batter making every base occupied and bringing up Fernando Tatis who then crushed a pitch thrown by starting pitcher, Chan Ho Park, into the left field bleachers for a grand slam home run, making the score 4-2 Cardinals. After a series of unusual events, the Cardinals once again loaded the bases with Tatis coming up to bat again with the bases loaded. The score at that time was 7-2 Cardinals against the same pitcher, Chan Ho Park (I have never understood just why he was still pitching), who hung a curve that Tatis crushed once again to the left field bleachers, very close to where the first grand slam ended. Two grand slams in the same inning! That never happened before in Major League Baseball and will probably never happen again, especially off the same pitcher! I asked both of my good friends, Jack Buck, the Cardinals broadcaster (who called both slams), and Marty Hendin (Vice President of the Cardinals) if that opportunity ever occurred before in a major league game, and they both doubted the possibility, especially off the same starting pitcher. Sensible thinking would dictate that after seven runs allowed by the starting pitcher, that pitcher would have been pulled before the opportunity presented itself once again. Without question, I firmly believe that is the only time it could possibly occur, and will probably never happen again, certainly against the same pitcher. The final score was 12-5 Cardinals.

I, as a baseball art photographer, had the exclusive rights to photograph Mark McGwire's seventieth home run baseball as well as Sammy Sosa's sixty-sixth home run baseball. I created a photo of each of those baseballs in a limited edition print. Therefore, I had a reason to make the following call the morning after Fernando Tatis hit those two grand slams in one inning. This fact was all over the news media, and a big, big deal. I called my gallery at the moment it opened. Darlene Williams, the gallery director, answered my call.

Using an accent that I tried to mimic of Fernando's, I said, "Hallo, ees Mr. Markaese dere?"

Darlene said, "No, I'm sorry he isn't, who is calling, please?"

"Deese ese Fernando Tatis."

"Oh, Mister Tatis, I am certain that Mr. Marquess would love to talk with you, why do you want to talk to him?"

In my strong Fernando Tatis accent, I said, "I want him to photograph my balls!"

There was a long pause and a complete silence for several moments when finally Darlene said, "Oh, Don, why do you do this to me?" And then laughed hysterically. As a matter of fact, I laughed a lot as well! I got her again.

Just another quick story about Darlene who was a very beautiful lady with a terrific sense of humor who could speak with anyone at their level, from a truck driver to a corporate executive. She was with Anheuser Busch at their world headquarters in St. Louis, and was an excellent lady for my gallery. She had that very rare talent to relate to any person entering the gallery and they all liked her immediately.

One morning, while driving to work, I saw a sign in front of Webster High School announcing Blood Drive Today. I called the gallery to speak with Darlene about various topics regarding sales of my prints, and at the end of the conversation, I told her that I had donated a pint of blood to the Red Cross for their blood drive.

She said, "Don, that is great."

I said that the nurse would be at the gallery at 4:00 p.m.

Darlene said, "OK, I'll see you then."

I said, "I will try to make it, but maybe not. I donated a pint of your blood, not mine!"

Once again, while laughing, "Oh, Don, why do you keep doing this to me?"

CHAPTER 39

Dogs Are Truly Man's Best Friend

As a pre-teen, I had my best friend, Sarge, a collie/mutt blend. My grandmother had a neighbor with a beautiful collie that looked just like the big TV star, Lassie, who just had a litter by some non-pedigreed vagabond who apparently saw the beautiful collie in the backyard, became enraptured with that collie's irresistible body, jumped the fence, and left his calling card. Itinerant dogs carry no papers, so it was just a drive-by impregnation. My grandmother told my mother that the lady across the street was selling these tainted puppies for $10 bucks each. My mom told me that if I wanted a marked down doggie, it would cost me $10. I had saved $16.50 from my paper route, so I had the pick of this embarrassing litter. Sarge was the best looking and most intelligent and friendly puppy of the litter, so he became mine!

Sarge was my constant companion with his white fur, brown ears, and a few brown markings with a fluffy collie tail. I bragged to my friends and created a story that I almost believed about a timber wolf being Sarge's daddy. Sarge was my bodyguard and best friend. I had a friend, Dick, and he and I rode our bikes almost everywhere with Sarge running alongside. Dick saw Sarge every day and felt very comfortable around him. One day, Dick left something accidentally on our dining room table. It was summer and hot as hell in the middle of July. The dining room window was partly open. Dick pushed it open and started to climb in. Bad idea. Sarge denied his entry, barked, snapped, and growled with a menacing tooth-baring snarl that made Dick reconsider entry. The next day, Dick told me about the encounter, but he and my guarding Sarge were close friends once again. Sarge knew his job as a house patrol officer, and as long as you didn't invade his protected responsibility, you were just fine.

In much later years, after being married to Susan for thirty years or so, we had a black and white Cocker Spaniel named Murphy that became my spiritual adviser. No matter what happened during the day in my business, I would come home, and Murphy was always happy to see me regardless of any of the bad happenings in my business, or in the world for that matter. Murphy was always thrilled and happy to see me. The stock market could take a major hit, but Murphy didn't seem to care. Murphy would jump on my lap. I could tell him my misfortunes, but he still had his very positive and very fun outlook. He always looked at me with an expression that said, "Hey, nothing matters. If I have you and my milk bone, what is there to worry about?" He always convinced me to look at the brighter side of life. Truly my spiritual adviser.

I have always loved Old English sheep dogs but have never owned one. It always seemed to me that it would be best if a neighbor owned one that I could visit from time to time. As luck would have it, our neighbor Art Tonkins had a loveable one named, Daisy, that was eternally a puppy. Even at eight years old, she had the temperament of an eight-month-old puppy. We developed a strong friendship though separated by our backyard fence.

Another kind of dog that I thought was beautiful but never knew the name of the breed—I described it and Susan told me it's name—was a Weimaraner. I really liked its short tannish brown coat that had a definite mauve tone, and I thought that was a definite artistic attribute. Also Weimaraners had a nose that matched the body. A Weimaraner's nose definitely made that breed a beauty. Luckily, Susan thought the same and did extensive research to find the perfect Weim pup. There was a breeder in Florida named Bagshaw Breeders, and they had a litter of pups that were for sale. The strain of Weimaraners that they had was called Magnum, and they were bred for temperament and size. We picked one from the photos they sent by FedEx and picked one with the most intelligent and friendly face. They flew our choice male to St. Louis, and we could not have chosen a better one. Although he was only five weeks old when we got him, he seemed to have an inner instinct that his bodily functions were for the backyard only. He *never* made a mess inside. We learned later that the Magnum strain meant *big*! Our cute little puppy that we named Toby grew to an incredibly powerful 118 lbs. He was one strong hunk of dog flesh. Every night when I came home from work, I would hold his rawhide chew bone and he, with his incredibly powerful jaws, would gnaw on it until my arms tired out. He was great with kids in the neighborhood, and Donny and Danny, our boys, loved him as well. We felt that little kids could almost ride on his back and would never feel in danger. Toby was indeed a gentle giant. However, bad guys, beware, he could remove an arm or two if provoked.

Toby had a strong conscience and was greatly remorseful if he did something wrong. At those rare times of infraction, he would get very low on the carpet, come toward me very apologetically, and plead with me with his amber eyes and beg for forgiveness. If Toby had something in his mouth that he thought might be frowned upon by us, he would take it to the dining room and hide in plain sight under the dining room table.

For our fifteenth anniversary, Susan gave me a beautiful Rolex Cellini watch that was eighteen carat gold with a beautiful brown leather band. I came out of the shower, and the vanity counter where I left it was bare. No Rolex. I went downstairs to the dining room, and there was Toby chewing away with the leather band hanging out of one side of his mouth. He had his guilty dog expression when he saw me, and stopped chewing, and allowed me to rescue my watch. One side of the watch leather band was gone and the other side with the clasp was slowly disappearing.

Toby allowed me to pry open his mouth and retrieve the watch. I managed to save the clasp, which was eighteen carat gold as well. The jeweler told me it was lucky I saved it because to replace it was over $120. Toby was guilty as hell as well as remorseful. I still have the reminder of his felony by a tooth mark on the backside of my watch. (At the time of his infraction, I was tempted to give him a memory of my tooth mark on his backside.)

When a service man would come to the house, Toby would place his 118 pound body between Susan and the serviceman, and just sit calmly on guard between them with the unspoken advice: "One false move, Buster, and you will regret it!"

I took Toby to see Dr. Clark at the Clark Animal Hospital for his annual checkup and the waiting room was packed. Toby was very well behaved, no matter where he was, and sat in front of me with his usual noble position with his chest in its normal kingly stance. All of the other dogs were sitting on the floor with their masters. Everything was under control in the waiting room. Then a man walked in with his coal black Scottish Terrier who proceeded to disrupt the peace and quiet of the waiting room, as he barked at every dog there, and then all of the dogs started barking and whining and total chaos erupted. Toby didn't change position, but very loudly let out a giant woof! All of the dogs, including the disturber Terrier, kind of bounced in the air, and total silence filled the room.

Toby was indeed a wonderful animal and my best friend for many years

Now Bella is our wonderful animal with a beautiful face, a great heart, and an insatiable appetite. When I come home, Bella is always happy to see me, and even happier if I have a treat for her, and I give her a ten-minute-or-so neck massage.

Dogs are just flat the greatest. They seem to love me just as I love them!

Chapter 40

Some People Can Tell a Joke, Some People Can't

Humor has a way of making a cloudy day sunny. I can be in a very down mood, but reading several pages of my collection of Gary Larson (the Far Side) cartoons, makes me feel much better. A Mel Brook movie can have the same effect. *Young Frankenstein* is one of the best ever. Humor indeed soothes the troubled soul. I am offering a few of my favorite humorous stories.

1. A man was doing an article on prison life and attended a large prison in central Kansas. He completed his morning tour and was invited to join the inmates for lunch. There may have been 150 or so inmates. After the meal, one of the inmates stood up and said very loudly, "Seventy-four!" and everybody laughed. Another man stood up and yelled, "Twenty-four!" then everyone laughed again. Then one other stood up and said loudly, "Twelve." The reporter asked the warden just what was going on.

127

The warden explained, "Most of these inmates have been here for a long time and have heard most of the jokes many, many times, and the lunch break is rather short, so they compiled a list of 150 of the funniest jokes they have ever heard. They wrote them all down and compiled them in a booklet, so in the interest of saving time, the inmates will just call out a number for their joke of choice instead of taking the time to tell the entire joke." The reporter was amazed and asked if he could read it and come back for dinner with the inmates in the dining hall. He was given the booklet and read all of the jokes and found the funniest one. He went to the dinner to join the inmates.

After dinner one man stood up and yelled, "Sixty-two." Everyone roared with laughter.

"Fifty-four," another yelled, then a hearty laughter erupted.

The reporter saw a pause, stood up, and yelled "Forty-six."

Dead silence, no one laughed at all.

Once again, he stood up and screamed even louder, "Forty-six!" Still no response. He told the warden, "I have read the entire list of jokes, and that one is the absolute funniest I have ever heard. I yelled it twice and no one laughed. Why?"

The warden said, "Well, some people can tell a joke . . . some people can't."

2. It was late at night when the phone rings in the army motor pool. The private answers the phone and says, "Motor Pool."

The voice says. "What is available in the pool tonight?"

The private says, "Four jeeps, a couple of pickups, and a big Cadillac for the fat-assed general."

The caller says very loudly, "Do you know who you are talking to?"

The private says, "No, I don't."

The voice says, "This is the general!"

The private says, "Who wee, do you know who you are talking to?"

The general says, "No, I don't."

The private then says, "Well, goodbye, fat ass!"

3. A very wealthy rancher went on a safari and was enraptured by the zebras. He thought they were the most incredible animals he had ever seen. He wanted to bring one back to his ranch. He arranged and purchased one, then brought her back and let her run freely in the meadow on his ranch.

    A bull noticed this new animal running around in the field, and walked up to the zebra and said, "What in the world are you doing on this ranch?"

    The zebra said, "Well, I am just supposed to run around here and look beautiful. What do you do around here?"

    The bull replied, "Take off those striped pajamas, and I'll show you!"

4. An elderly man and his wife were taking their daily walk and noticed that a new insurance company had opened in their local shopping center.

    The wife says to the husband, "You know, Charlie, maybe you should think about getting some life insurance."

    He said, "You know, you are probably right, let's go and check it out."

    They walk into the office, and Charlie's wife sits in the waiting room, while the husband goes in to talk to the agent.

    He says to the agent, "I am considering purchasing a life insurance policy, what will it cost?"

The agent looks at the obviously very old man and says, "I don't know, sir, how old are you?"

Charlie says, "I am ninety-two years old, but I feel great. My wife and I take a walk every day, I mow the lawn every week and shoot baskets with friends of mine every Sunday afternoon. The old ticker is in great shape!"

The agent says, "Do you have a doctor?"

"Of course I do"…

"What is your doctor's name?'"

Charlie says, "My doctor's name, my doctor's name . . . my doctor's name . . . what is that flower that has a long stem with thorns and beautiful red petals?"

The agent says, "Rose?"

"Rose, that's right. Rose! What's my doctor's name?"

5. Dave, up in years, calls his doctor and says, "Doc, I am feeling great and I have fully recovered from that cardiac incident I had months ago, and Margie and I greatly miss those intimate moments we used to have. Is it possible to have a prescription for Viagra?"

Doc says, "I don't think that is wise, Dave, you know you have just recently recovered from your heart incident."

"But, Doc, Margie and I really miss those intimate moments together . . . Please, Doc!"

"OK, Dave, but let's do it this way, take Viagra for a week, skip a week, take Viagra another week, skip another week, then call me."

Weeks go by and Dave doesn't call, so the doctor gets worried and calls his number. Margie answers and the doctor says, "Margie, how is Dave?"

"Oh, Doc, I am so sorry, Charlie died last week."

The doctor says, "It was the Viagra, wasn't it?"

"No, Doc. It was all that skipping."

6. A man was sitting on an airplane next to a very well dressed elderly lady, and as the sun caught the ring on her finger the reflection of it was almost blinding. The man kept looking at the incredible diamond and just had to ask about it. He said, "Ma'am, I am a jeweler in Manhattan and I have never seen such an incredible diamond, it looks almost as big as the Hope Diamond."

She says, "Yes, it is almost the same size, it is the Klopman Diamond, but like the Hope Diamond, it carries a curse."

The jeweler says, "A curse? What is the curse?"

She says "Mr. Klopman."

7. After Quasimodo fell to his death, Notre Dame was in the market for a new bell ringer. So posters were put out with the notice. After several days, a man applied who had no arms and wanted the job. He told the man in the bell tower that Quasimodo was a hero to him, and he wanted the job as bell ringer out of respect for him.

"But how can you do that? You have no arms," he said.

"I'll show you."

He backed up to the door started running toward the bell, smashed it with his face, slipped and fell out the window, and crashed to his death on the ground. A crowd gathered around as the custodian ran downstairs and one of the crowd said to him, "Who is he?"

"I don't know, but his face rings a bell."

Two days later another applicant comes to the bell tower and asks for the job. He said that his armless brother fell to his death last week, and out of respect for his brother, he wanted the job.

The custodian said, "OK, let's see how you do."

The man backed up to the door and took off at great speed, grabbed the rope on the bell, his hands slipped, and he tumbled to his death on the ground below. The custodian ran down the stairs and a crowd had gathered around and asked him who the dead man was.

He replied, "I don't know, but he is a dead ringer for his brother!"

(Sorry about that one)

8. Sidney and his wife of ten years were invited to a party, and Sid says to his wife, Sarah, "Now these are guys that I play poker with every Wednesday, and they are bringing their wives, so just be nice. Please, don't start making up stories to make you sound important, just be a nice person and listen."

After a wonderful evening with great food and friends, they get back in the car, and as soon as the door closes, Sidney says, "Well, Sarah, you did it again! The subject of classical music came up and they started talking about Mozart. You had to jump in the conversation and say, "'Oh, Mozart was such a nice young man, we met and talked at the Fifty-Seventh Street subway station many, many times,' and you kept talking about it and repeated it many times! How could you be so dumb? You know the train doesn't stop on Fifty-Seventh!"

9. A nice, young Jewish boy comes home after graduating from college with a degree in economics. And he says, "Mom, I got a job offer and I am working for Jesus."

The mom almost faints and says, "Oh no, my son . . . How could you do that after all your fine and educational times at the temple and in this kosher household?"

He says, "Don't get excited, Mama . . . Kraft Jesus, Kraft Cheeses!"